Inward Reflections

Poetry and Quotes from the Heart

Dr. Suman Lata Vohra Vermani

INDIA · SINGAPORE · MALAYSIA

ISBN 979-8-89544-802-1

My creative writing is motivated by the legendary

Gurudeva Swami Paramhansa Yogananda ji

This book *'Inward Reflections – Poetry and Quotes from the Heart'* is dedicated to Him

My Parents Late Smt. Santosh and Sh.
Rajinder L Vohra, My Ultimate Role Models

This book *'Inward Reflections – Poetry and
Quotes from the Heart'* is a tribute to them 🏵

Blessings

ഔ൰

My Maternal Uncle (Mamaji) Sri Rajinder K Kapur, who always encouraged me for my creative work 🪔

'Where words fail, music speaks. So true and yet not so true'

Dr. Suman Lata, holding a PhD in Music, also a distinguished faculty member in the Music and Dance Department of Kurukshetra University, has lived and breathed music throughout her life. However, a new chapter has unfolded in her journey, leading her to awaken her latent talents as a poetess. Gifted with the ability to excel in both realms of music and poetry, she has truly found her artistic balance.

Suman's artistic talent has seamlessly transcended from the rhythms of music to the graceful rhythm of words in her poems. Her literary contributions include two volumes of Hindi lyrical poetry: *Sumanmala* and *Geet Vinyas*, both of which are in circulation. A third book, *Man Ki Vani* has also been published.

Now, introducing her first collection of lyrical English poetry and quotes, *Inward Reflections – Poetry and Quotes from the Heart*, Suman showcases her linguistic versatility. Her command over both Hindi and English poetry is a testament to her exceptional skills, deserving admiration and applause.

Set yourself free, like a butterfly, and the flight of imagination takes over. As the renowned poet Robert Frost stated, "Poetry is when an emotion has found its thoughts and the thoughts have found its words".

That's precisely what my gifted niece Suman has achieved through her new book *Inward Reflections – Poetry and Quotes from the Heart*. This collection invites all poetry enthusiasts to experience the splendour of nature, love, loyalty, sincerity, spirituality, and the various aspects of life.

Inward Reflections – Poetry and Quotes from the Heart resonates with the harmonious union of mind and heart, a creation nurtured by Suman's inner self. This collection is destined to touch the hearts of countless lovers of lyrical poetry.

With my blessings, love and best wishes.

Rajinder K Kapur

Assistant Director (Retd) O and M Services,

Customs and Central Excise, Delhi

Sh. Rajinder K Kapur dedicated the last 38 years of post-retirement serving the poor, needy and underprivileged sections of society. Still active at the age of 95 years as President, People's Welfare Society, Ambala City.

Index

QUOTES 161

Preface

ಇಾಅ

Creative thoughts originated in my mind
I write my emotions clearly, in a different kind
And create atmosphere with sensory language
Aura and sound I would like my readers to imagine

In this chaotic and contradictory world, I've found a harmonious way to engage in compassionate, rhythmic actions that bring me joy. I aim to touch my soul by transforming my mind into an aura of positivity. I only wish I could be certain that it was the right thing to become a part of nature and hold the Universe in my hands and mind. The pleasing collection of emotional groundwork in style embodies the confidence that matters most. In my opinion, poetry is the best way to express feelings and emotional consciousness clearly. The format of *Inward Reflections - Poetry and Quotes from the Heart* tales on a lyrical form of self-expression. Its subject is the viewpoint of feelings and the sound of silence. The poetry represents the version of myself. I delve into simple words, and the spectrum of my emotional lyrics flows out onto the page. My most intense obsession brings out a clear picture of my life, love, loyalty, sincerity and spirituality. So, I nurture ideas in my mind map by infusing truth into the words and actions of my unique thoughts, poems speak for themselves. I ensure that I preface as just a reflection of myself.

My aim for writing is to highlight poems on various subjects using different terms and prompted by different feelings, using the best words in the best order. Actually, it's a part of both my head and heart. My brain generates classified ideas, makes decisions, and writes. I discard all useless thoughts and develop a personal vision of the One, my beloved God, and spend time in His elevating company, which boosts my self-esteem more than any other can do. Whatever has happened to me in my life, luckily, I have the ability to transform my feelings into a poetic language, and my journey through life so far clearly proves that.

Well, read this collection cover by cover and meet me in a mind map of words, ideas and tasks within this *Inward Reflections - Poetry and Quotes from the Heart*, where the silent voice speaks and presents a good story of my authenticity and passion with the rhythmic words of my purposeful life. It's a gift to myself and to my world. Therefore, it's necessary to share myself with the rest of the world. The complete picture shows my attitude and inner approach to my *Inward Reflections – Poetry and Quotes from the Heart*. I hope you will cherish my rhythmic world of words and the sound of silence. Keep reading to learn more.

Dr. Suman Lata Vohra Vermani

Reviews

'Inward Reflections - Poetry and Quotes from the Heart' is a language of the heart and soul, of the emotions and feelings set deep inside.

Dr. O P Vermani

Professor (Retd)

NIT Kurukshetra

One can easily sense the fragrance of paper, indicating that a lot is going on in the poetess's heart. She subtly mentions just a little bit of things of life silently on a page. Ideally each word is charged with emotions and rhythmically well-organised.

Dr. Arun Khosla

Professor

NIT Jalandhar

'Inward Reflections - Poetry and Quotes from the Heart' is a complete little universe in itself. The writer listens to her inner voice and transforms it into poetic language. The rehearsal of emotions and sensations are embodied in the words.

Dr. Mamta Khosla

Professor

NIT Jalandhar

ℋ

'Inward Reflections - Poetry and Quotes from the Heart' has strong settings. Outlined ways and ideas are well explored in style, offering concrete insights into life.

Gagan Vermani

CEO and Founder of MySun Noida

ℋ

In her lyrical poetry, she emphasises that her verses are a part of her mind and brain that is powered by layers of feelings and emotional actions.

Prerana Vermani

Teacher, Lotus Valley International School, Noida

ℋ

As a lyrical writer, she resides on her own planet and expresses her entire life. She provides a perspective while lying in bed at night, thinking what she really thinks and writes to comfort her own solitude with fitting and pleasing words. She gets entrapped in her heart; a wide range of words come to her through the Divine Grace of God.

Dr. Malika Ahuja

Germany

⅍

In this 'Inward Reflections - Poetry and Quotes from the Heart' the emotional world of words is totally content with its silent sound. Makes sure that is captivating enough to arouse curiosity.

Vikas Ahuja

Software Engineer, Germany

⅍

A gifted artist who has done justice to both—music and poetry. From the rhythm of music to the beautiful flow of words in poems.

Lalit Kapur

GM Commercial at Air India (Retd)

Former Senior Management at Air India Delhi.

Acknowledgements

ॐ

First of all, I would like to thank Goddess Sarasvati for Her grace. She is undoubtedly the only presence in this Universe that has guided me and enhanced vibrations of my thoughts, work, and actions within my heart, mind, and brain. I humbly bow down to this divine grace with the following mantra:

या देवी सर्वभूतेषु विद्या रूपेण संस्थिता।

नमस्तस्यै नमस्तस्यै नमस्तस्यै नमो नमः॥

Next, I express my heartfelt appreciation and thanks to my son in law, Dr. Arun Khosla, Professor at NIT Jalandhar. He has encouraged, motivated and inspired me to promote my lyrical emotions onto paper. His unwavering support has been an incredible source of inspiration. I cannot express in words how he has generously dedicated his precious time for me, shaping the present work into what it is. I offer my deep sense of gratitude to my daughter, Dr. Mamta Khosla, also a Professor in NIT Jalandhar, who encouraged me to the highest peak of guidance.

I am truly thankful to my son, Gagan Vermani, CEO and founder of 'My Sun' Solar Company in Noida, for his unwavering moral support. I must acknowledge my daughter-in-law, Prerana Vermani, for her valuable guidance.

I am greatly indebted to my younger daughter Dr. Malika Ahuja, for her understanding and continuous encouragement. I am greatly obliged to my younger son-in-law Vikas Ahuja, a software engineer in Germany, for his elevating inspiration.

I record my gratitude towards my companion, Dr. O P Vermani, a retired Professor from NIT Kurukshetra, for his helpful discussions and encouragement.

My thanks are due to my grandson Paras Khosla, Ishaan Vermani, Ojas Ahuja, Gurvansh Vasu Khosla and granddaughters Pavani Ahuja and Tulip Vermani for their love and encouragement.

A special thanks to my grandsons Paras Khosla, Ishaan Vermani, Ojas Ahuja and granddaughter Pavani Ahuja who have consistently aided and encouraged me in preparing the perfect document presentation.

Although the presentation of my *Inward Reflections - Poetry and Quotes from the Heart* is a result of my personal efforts, it would not have been possible without the kind support and help of many individuals. I have no valuable words to express my sincere appreciation and gratitude, but my heart is still full of the favours received from each and every person.

I am also an incredible inspiration to myself, and I express my gratitude for that as well.

          ACKNOWLEDGEMENTS

At last, but not the least, I admit one great fact that my beloved Guru Shri Paramhansa Yogananda's blessings played a key role in the completion of this text. Without His blessings, this text could not have become a reality.

Dr Suman Lata Vohra Vermani

POEMS

Within My Heart

ॐ

Within my heart my Guru has a special place
God created him in His wisdom and in His grace
I bestow a high honour on my spiritual teacher
His teachings shape my world a better, wiser place

He gives me aura of profound ideas of awareness
So, I can transmit aesthetic intensity of self-reliance
He reflects a sense of confidence ability and serenity
And fills my body, mind, soul with the waves of ecstasy

My faith in my beloved Guru, by the minute, grows deeper
He enhances vibration of ideas clearly in my world inner
In the darkness of my life, he is a ray of light all around
My creative writing is motivated by legendary preacher

My Parents

ഇൻ

My parents sacrificed so much to get me where I am today
Their deep devotion is endless and enduring, come what may

Every moment of their happiness for my joy which they gave
Hid all tensions, problems, from me, used to say it's all okay

Their moments, actions, abilities, were specific with ideal way
Instilled idealism in me, my ultimate Role Models, are they

Throughout inspirational supportive role for raising me they play
They made me stand in the storm of life and showed the right way

Their efforts and love in raising me, I appreciate every day
Their involvement, a key so grave, to my success, their love they gave

Ability to speak to others in a self-assured, persuasive, toning way
I owe everything to my parents, they raised me up in such a way

 INWARD REFLECTIONS

Next to God, the title of my parents is the greatest in every way
What they have done for me timely, I will never be able to repay

What I am is because of them, a wiser individual person today
How to acknowledge my gratitude to them, I have no words to say

True Meaning of Life

୫୬

Often whenever on my couch I lie
Ask myself a question what is life
Who I truly am, from where do I come
What am doing here, I am here why

I've to face unbearable injuries why
Every moment new experience why
I close my eyes take a deep breath
Relax, nobody knows the answer why

Be alert enough, think deep inside
Make sure, you're in the class of life
For finding something just to live for
To improve the quality of entire life

Life is really to be experienced high
Embrace yourself, you are free to fly
Be you and do your best as you can
Achieving yourself is worth being alive

Be true to you, and give life your best,
To achieve yourself, a worthy quest.
Living fully is what life's about,
In every moment, cast away doubt

Purpose of life is whatever you ascribe
Being alive is the deep meaning of life
Certainly, it's so obvious, simple so plain
Essence of my being compels me to write

What I Feel

What I feel, can say about my wonderful life
The very essence of my being I want to describe

Close enough to earth and have a tendency to fly
Which makes me feel much free, elevated alike

Mind catches glimpse out of the corner of my eye
Glimpses of visible moments give me hint in order to write

Life Moves Round and Round

Life moves round and round with swings and slide
We move, that is the amazing ability to still alive

Learn to get in touch with your true self awhile
Focus on the good attitude and moral actions of life

Embrace life's calm in the little things you find,
Listen to your inner voice, let it guide your mind

Make a chamber of valuable smart ideas inside
Colour it with loveliness all around beauty alive

Life is about creating our experiences in artistic style
Art for Art's sake: That is the real aim of every life

Write in your heart that each day is the best day of life
It must be the most precious priority of your life

It is you who creates your life with your fashioned style
Keep striving for efforts to be better for peaceful life

Be a 'Branded Star' Suman! in your own unique style
By your example, others will be also inspired high

Life is Full of Challenges

ಬಂಡ

Life is always full of challenges and trials
But everyone perceives it in a different style

Some learn to live with things that happen in life
Some change the challenges by charismatic style

Some look for the experiences of being alive
Some enjoy the wonders and beauty of life

My challenging situation I take a deep breath and smile
It's God's grace to strengthen me to rise

My Life

෨෦෨

My life has been always full of problems
But I love living it and letting it be awesome

So whatever life offers I accept it anyway
Being a strong person I act like I'm okay

Even though tears in eyes I wear big smile
I do so with my patience and tackle my life

I know, no problem is here to stay forever
So, I let it go, do meditation and stay happier

Why You Seek

Why you seek questions of yourself for answers outside
When all the answers are hidden in the book of your life

Take a glance and seek, you will find a new power of life
A whole new fascinated world of glimpses inside

Trust your intuition and follow your heart's advice
There is nothing more powerful than the power inside

Make your concept clear, just see with your inward eye
You will be rewarded with more fantastic answers of life

God has Created this Earth

੪੨

God has created this earth as a place to live and love here
Understand the beauty of real joy, faith and truth here

It's a blessed life to know it, to feel it and to improvise here
You're not on this earth for worry, tension, stress and fear

Be a very real human being, give a meaning of humanity here
Pass the light of peace and love, and sing God's glory here

Take an honest look of your stylish life on each step here
Oh my dear! Beauty in own self lies in becoming self-aware

With the power of magnetic virtue, breathe freely in your native air
Be a human being of substance: Say Goodbye to fear

Silently

❀

When the whole world is sinking in sound sleep
I elevate my soul mind and body with divinity deep

It's a beauteous night absolutely calm and free
This quiet time brings pleasant sensations to me

I am delightful in solitude and sing to cheer up me
I love to do my work silently, only God's eyes can see

When You Do Something Wrong

 හංඃ

When you do something wrong, your whole being cries
That is the voice of God, within you to guide

If you do not listen to that voice, God remains quite
When you improve yourself, and strive to realize

Then God will help you and show the way right
Whatever you do good or bad, after all you're His child

My Heart is a Temple of Love

I decorate it with the lovable blossoms of joyous quality
I flirt with the understanding of all scented buds of humility

My romantic dreams generate me in such simplicity
I engage myself with the blooms of free spirit actually

My heart permits me to marry with the liberty of generosity
I divorce egoism and live a bountiful life joyously

True Hope

True hope swiftly flies with the wings

Ever rests in the soul, in silent sound sings

Keeps on moving forward in winter warm springs

It's the only assurance, you can trust your instincts

Gives countless chances to make right things

It's the Hope nurtures faith in the mind of human beings

Take Care

Take care of each breath you take
Cherish each moment with shield of faith

Today is the only life, so try to best make
you're a branded star, Dear! you just shake

Be you, be free, It's necessary for you to awake
Let your priority up, in your own unique way

My Perspective of Sky

೮೦೦೪

For oft when on my chair I sit and look at the sky
It seems to be a pure cooler blue peaceful sky

I look the shade of orange during sunset and sunrise
That gives me hope, the sun sets only to again rise

And adds so many smiling colours of nature into my life
That give worth of jewel shine to enhance my inner life

Clouds come floating to carry rain into my dreamy life
Vast azure in rainbow clouds look so pearly so flamy bright

A complete balanced harmony is the principle of light
I'm looking for what will next be to keep my eyes

The surface of wider horizon bounded by propitious sky
I make in my mind a new horizon for my healthy eyes

What a contemplate the glory of God beyond describe
The whole nature is listed under the one whole sky

Everything exists under the law of cosmic surprise
Galaxies forming thick network look like human brain alive

I'm always been fascinated between the two worlds of sky
Beautiful sparkling with diamonds the starry night

Mornings radiate with various colours and well-ordered life
All human beings and nature relaxing in the perfection of sky

To look over the vastness of sky and see the smallness of I
The measureless space of marbled sky : O' GOD is art Thy

I'm nothing God Thou art fills the place where am I
Whatever I'm, the life force of your Universe Infinitely high

Sometimes it makes sense that God is staring me up high
Opening for me a clear 'God's Career ' with rhythmic style

I love to watch the 'Infinite movie' across the sky
I'm on the way, on line! Look at me, Hey dear Sky

Life is a Battlefield

Life is a battlefield and the real battle is within us
Million times by emotional bullets, we're badly hurt

Not so much by others but by armed foes of own thoughts
Every time God and devil are fighting within our hearts

Our natural elasticity is crushed by the devil armed corps
Everyone in this world is burdened with problematic faults

But there is so much to know that we're inwardly good sorts
So we need to charge this feeling by honourable upshots

Much in life we can achieve by skilful use of crafts
I trust, we can, put devil off in putting off from inside a parts

And only the spark of pure spirits will remain long lost
O' Lord! Give me strength to win through devotional skill sharps

The valour with great ferocity and intensity of my troops across

So I may live by confidence and faith in love of God

And improve inter balancing energetic field of life at large

Yet with the courage of a spiritual Hero and with joyful sparks

If I Were a Bird

෫෬

If I were a bird, I'd fly freely on high
My life would be a beautiful blend of fly

I would be slanted on the wind, when it comes by
And would take me away where I wanted to fly

I would use the wings of flying Universe to touch the sky
And watch the earth from up above so high

Everything would look tiny from up that sky
Sea, buildings, people, vehicle would be small in size

I would travel the world, wherever whenever enjoy my ride
Even in storms, rains, snows, I would be able to fly

By touching the clouds, I would enjoy an air borne life
And wear the rainbow garment, for me to beautify

I would go through north-south, east-west, a cool adventurous life
spread my balanced wings, and fly as high on high

When I'd get down below, then wave with smile
To be delighted within, get up again and sing "I Love You Sky"

In darkness I would dream dreams with open eye
It would be an amazing experience of my life

Join Me

Join me on my journey to pack each day
Fill it with worthwhile activities anyway

For mental physical hygiene with pure mind pray
Find the road of inner peace on the infinite way

Sing the song of God's glory in rhythmic way
Serve happiness to everyone you meet on the way

Spread the light of love like the sun ray
Thus make journey harmonious along the way

Learn to Get in Touch

Learn to get in touch with your true self awhile
Recognise yourself for who you're truly deep inside

Your authentic uniqueness is filled with joy and smile
God's blessings are the remote of your charming life

Behold the beauty of love, see the happier side of life
Colour it with lovely attractive harmony all around alive

Click on various images, enjoy and let life be your guide
You're the song, sing for others and for your sake awhile

You are the guide and guardian of all your moral being alive
What's right for you 'Suman', only your true self can decide.

To Strive

ॐ

To strive, to seek, to find is an art
Get up and start doing with a heart
Wheresoever you may turn day night
Dreaming mind must be a proud part

Root yourself in love and humanity
Feed your heart with joyful loyalty
This broad world is a field of battle
Be a hero in this strife full reality

Either I May

৪০৫৪

Either I may go left or right, you just turn at beauteous glance aside
And watch my dancing feet, try not to dance with me nor
hold awhile

To see the moving art of my spirit, you just give a big
mesmerizing smile
Each word is a movement of my feet, it's the poetry of my
dancing style

Feel the technique of my expression and natural order of
joyous inside
My body language is a gift of communication between soul
and my life

Happiness is Love

Happiness and Love has very close Connection
Sweetness of love creates deep happiness within

Both are interconnected with the aroma of inspiration
And the top most priorities of mental physical condition

It's a valuable blessing and priceless gift from Heaven
The basic reservoir of energy like blood of natural evolution

The whole world needs; it's the greatest possession
'Happiness is love' full stop free flow of God's expansion

My Universe

౸౹౸

Standing at the top a wide
Open roof of sky everywhere
It has connection with the earth with
A sign of livelihood for sure

Everyone is moving below on the majestic
floor of sky here
The whole world is charged with the
Heavenly great powers here

And using all resources of life given
to us as a gift here
People get what they desire every
grace of God's care

Life between Earth and Sky makes

A sense of living fair

I bow to the Sky and Earth, They're

the Chief of all Empire

My Unique Kind

౸ൟ൧

When I turn over my eye on the book of my life line
Nothing rewarding for my any struggle I find

Unpleasantness scratched deeply by moving all the time
Still focused on priorities for myfuture line

I aligned all activities with the clear vision of mine
All possibilities and solutions are within reach of mine

I'm well equipped to handle all challenges behind
And raised the bar for life by the power of my mind

My ultimate goal is to create a beautiful life Divine
Now I deliberately read again properly pages of past time

Wow Suman ! What a purposeful living marked all over behind
I calmly feel, It's a delightful authentic story of my unique kind

Proud to Be Me

I am proud to be me as the way I am
How you see me, I don't give a damn

I live love and look at my life in my way
I feel out flourish myself in a dignified way

I have my family and friends who love me
That love is more than enough for me to be

Leading a real authentic life with confidence
That is the true essence of inside naturalness

My attitude is simple original sophisticated
I focus on creativity by my ideas elaborated

I follow my heart and concentrate on my mind
Create my world in a way of being pretty kind

Literally the intensity of ideas of my headlines
Through lyrics story enter the land of lifelines

I am the relating writer of the script of my life
I am playing the part in the picture I set aside

I've come into the world to improve something
To love and be loved is the extraordinary thing

I don't think lot about my economic situation
My mental state is good to be content within

Life is a precious gift that we get it only once
It's beautiful with novelty of new experience

I'm sorry, I'm not, never will be a perfect person
Being myself I am ok in my perfect imperfection

I love being me, no one can dare to bow me down
I tell keep your judgement at bay, no more question

The Roof of Sky

౭౦౧౭

I gazed up above in the blue sky all around
How beautiful is the roof of sky, so soft so grand

From the floor I appreciate its pleasantness and calm sound
Dear God, I want to touch it by raising up above my hand

I'm wandering, how to reach up with my strong stand
Oh' my God, I scream with joy to feel a touch of sky land

My Heart is Filling with Delight

My heart is filling with delight nearer to the sea

The roaring water is calling my name with glee

My heart is filling with delight nearer to the sea

Winds are longing to play with my spirit gently

To the core of my childlike heart cheering up me

My heart is filling with delight nearer to the sea

In the midst of waves dancing, I set my spirit free

My heart is gone with the waves far, far from me

My heart is filling with delight nearer to the sea

Social Settings

All human beings are inherently made in social settings
Life comes from staying connected and ultimate getting

Oft the amount of social time we spend in social netting
And share freely our feelings in order to keep connecting

The channel of communication is receptive key of bonding
With people in various ways at various stage of sounding

Some of them are adored by well-bred pleasing chattering
Some of them are manipulative boring deceitful disgusting

I am at a point in my life where I have peacefulness within
I go along with those whose moral ideas are quite elevating

Cheerful Person

Cheerful person is an evergreen tree
Showering comfort and shelter free

A prized possession everyone wants to keep him relatively
A long spring of season yearned by one and all of his
humanity

Cheerful person is an evergreen tree
Showering comfort and shelter free

Such a loving being is my life line has childlike inner beauty
His cheerful attitude promotes my health ethics and morality

Cheerful person is an evergreen tree
Showering comfort and shelter free

He awakes each day with smile and emits a ray of positivity
Actually cheerfulness is a festival, what God made him to be

Cheerful person is an evergreen tree
Showering comfort and shelter free

Agility is a Mentality

ॐ

Agility is a mind-set, a joyful pursuit of activity
Spirit moves with ethical qualities naturally

God grants such souls with charming amiability
Based on different elements of cultural diversity

That can bring heaven on this earth probably
If adopted by one and all mind-sets of capability

Noisy World

There are too much voices in this noisy world
We need to hear symphony of peace in our heart

Sit quietly to hear our own unique authentic voice
Amazing sounds of peace singing in side of all of us

Once we hold onto turn down the noise of our mind
A fascinated sweet feeling of inner voice we can find

Let us make a goal to wrap our life in self-realization
By embracing a fashionable style of deep meditation

A straight door way of divine graceful friend pleasing
Listen clearly the voice of God through silence with in

Every moment God's voices resonate in the universe
We can hear if we tune our mind with inner universe

Let us take time to hear HIS voices by paying attention
And evoke HIS blessings of regular rhythm of daily living

Welcome to the Supernatural World

ॐ

Welcome to the supernatural world of divine romance

I think the price of admission is:

You'll get a silent cave of awareness

Sprinkling joy and peace nearby

Understanding and constant experience

The simple attitude of inner beauty

That comes as a result with poetic imagination

Life becomes a romantic song of lyrics

Rhythmically with the Eternal One, begins romance

Quiet Often

৪১৫৪

Quiet often sitting all alone on my cushioned bed
Suddenly so many ideas come through my head
To be sit alone in room it makes me feel so good
Loneliness calls me, let's write on the blank pad

As far as each word gives nice sort of substance
Approach of my ideas enshrine good sentence
I manifest ability being levelled in my confidence
A view of poetry is implicit in poems elements

Rhythmic composition set the scene of concepts
Ideas make over a polished way of life to it self
The aura and authenticity speaks my inner facts
poetry is a divine revelation of the self to the self

I Like to Write

৪৩

I like to write, write, write and write
Writing is what makes me feel delight

For me it's a spiritual way of self-realizing
I love spending rest of my time in writing

Honestly, that leads me to constant peace
I feel an exhaustless source of Supreme bliss

Really, it's so wonderful so inspirational to me
I get in tune with inner my voice so kind to me

Breathing of my heart catches word after word
With thoughtful reflection on myself and world

As far words give a sense and life to what I feel
By writing ultimate reality of my vision I reveal

I know, just a limited time on earth I have got
Like I am breathing today, tomorrow it will lost

When I will be no more on this glorious world
How amazing, I will be still alive in my text word

Keep talking to reader through rhythmic rhyme
Thus, my creative vision would last for a life time

I Am Born this Way

When I sit quietly to produce some writing art work
I give myself permission to get stuck with the word

In a simple way I express my feelings on blank paper
So that words should stick in the mind of reader clear

Silently I develop my distinctive voice in my own style
My writing voice reveals the deep reflection of my life

Readers should be able to hear sound of the contents
My abandon truest concepts well shaped in sentences

I try to make sense by engaging in the version of word
Keep on writing more, its God's voice leads me to work

Seriously I don't want my life may run in an ordinary way
So in a way my each word tells me that I'm born this way

My Best Mate

ഔ

A poem to me is like my best mate
I am in fact blessed by great fate
With whom I can share my feelings
Well for me, it's my spot of solace

Who allows me to pick up my pen
And write out on blank paper then
Whatever I hold in my curious mind
Put into best words in best order I can

It keeps on moving in my head always
For seizing and storing up in phrases
Remains until all held together by words
Thus create a new universe of my images

Poem is an origin of language state
Numberless ideas exist overly activate
It's a ground of shapes, forms and pace
inner feelings I may adequately articulate

Poem speaks to me inside of my heart
Putting self in to writing is a creative art
You find words from a small piece of land
Gonna applying it by communicating thought

I Am a Poem

ೱ∞

I am a poem, I am my page
My emotions are roller stage
rhythmic feet walk in the poem
With an evident display of craze

As ever poem walks down the page
Trapping of metre measure the pace
Pace moves the pulse of poem speed
It's need for the poem to get engaged

My Little Universe

Poetry is my little universe in it I make my own world
At last, here I find myself take playful rhythmic words
In fact, it's all my mind matter subjected to me directly
Happening in my life and my surrounding I write usually

I am one of many who writes rhythmic poetry everyday
It seems like a game so I love doing writing for to play
I just let my words maintain discipline to make a sound
String them together so they may express as best on ground

I shape them mould them as I play with solemn words
In this lonely ground, words are everything my world
Some people say, writing is a waste of time without pay
But I play for my pleasure it's all that I need to win day

I Am in Love

Oh' I am in love with writing rhythmic rhyme
This literary attitude of mine is always in prime

Writing spirit comes from my musical education
So there is a musical imperative in my sensation

In my choice I look for rhythm and tone in verse
Almost in classic style of rhythmic beauty in words

The words of my heart hints at the story to come
The main layers of my emotions comes to action

Rhyming words with sentences set a beautiful poem
Inter play of my feelings evoke metre and rhythm

I keep rhyming and post them into an inter net site
Without any literary fame, reward or pay I do write

It's an enjoyable hobby to me, in truth I can say
It brings inner joy, for me too hard to give away

I write rhymes because there's a voice with in me
I feel, ooh' it's my love of rhymes speak love for me

Blessed is the Man

ॐ

Blessed is the man who is delighted in the law of the Lord
Day and night he meditates on to HIS supreme law of holiness
Always puts God first, trusts Him, God too remains in him richly

He sings spiritual songs with gratitude in his heart
All that he is by divine grace, lives, loves, laughs with faith
He has the full measure of joy and peace within him completely

For him divine grace is sufficient, worth greater than gold
God watches over the way of his devoted gentleness
To his glorious richness, God meets all his need accordingly

He achieves a spiritual realisation it fills his soul with ecstasy
He loves God and his dedication towards HIM is great
Thus he celebrates life, says 'Thank you' cheers to God gracefully

Songs of Love

ೞ

Songs of love can never grow in pots
They can only grow inside of hearts

The rhythm of delicate hearts vibrates as one
Emotions flow when they sing songs of passion

They listen their sighs and tempt with their eyes
They hold each other and dance with smiles

For in love with one another they find peace
Perfect harmony in their lyrics, sweet release

In the Garden

ഔറ

In the garden of my mind, so many ideas I grow
And nurture feelings with coloured rays of rainbow

By putting truth in the words of my unique thoughts
Bring out the clear picture of my emotions to show

In so many shapes and forms of artistic expression
Delicate and tough words start its course to flow

When I make sure that the skin of words sound okay
Then I crystallize the beauty of its constructive glow

It's my way of connecting with myself by writing
Literary techniques authorise my polished concepts
to extend hello

I Encourage Me

I encourage me to play with the words entire
This way I press out project of emotional treasure

Writing emotions on paper helps me feel relaxed
A great therapy and the most fulfilling stress reliever

This way I please my heart and celebrate with me
That shines play list of my experience more brighter

Emotions into Words

Emotions into words it's my own feeling
Full of sweet and bitter twist, I am listing

Synopsis of my emotional history illustrating
My profound ideas lead me to translating

On paper all secret contents are penetrating
Lo, just in sentences emotional depth enhancing

Now is the time to greet my work by singing
Look at my work. O God, it's all your blessing.

The Way

The way I spend a lot of my precious time
Putting the pen in writing I feel so much fine

Just a little of little version of my thoughts
I dip my emotions onto simple paper white

Just like x-rays words come in to my head
By putting on page I feel most connected alive

Sometime I feel my emotions are at the peak
At that time I shake off everything as I write

Actually I meditate on my mind by writing
Look at miracles! My soul flows out in order to write

Intense obsessions are a fuel of my writing skill
I tell my poems, it's my own way to survive

Poem

Poem to me is 'to feel to self' into the words of rhythmic rhyme
A view of words elements displaying content obviously sublime

I look my poem as an art in which aesthetic intensity is adorning
Spill my soul of flowing feelings by tipping ink cartridge pouring

It takes shape of hidden feelings, tell version of my curious mind
Turn the page to see hear what do poems under current of sound

I write poems at that moment when loneliness comes calling me
I play with words hear the sound of mental rhythm inside of me

I try to formulate impression in rhythmic words in specific way
That please ears and touch heart's corner based on inter play

Each poem is closely tied with rhythm that is echo of my heart

Some evoke sorrow some evoke peace love joy make stress half

To get stuck with ideas is pleasant experience of being absorbed

An articulate rhythmic sound of words by rehearsal of thoughts

I Find a Way

I just have found a way of expressing my emotions inside

What I cannot say in words through rhymes I describe

For me it's exciting and easy to enjoy thought pattern

Words of mind and concepts become icons of inner eye

As I embark upon the journey to my rhythmical rhymes

It takes me further in to the world of peaceful sublime

Here none can interfere, I get me from myself to myself

I talk with images by help of words to bring my story to life

Writing is all about finding sound of words and create rhythm

I always feel music when I fill page with my heart breathing

I entertain writing visual and aural description of experience

I celebrate one life to live on beats that do align to my vision

Therapy

Writing lyrics has always been my therapy
That makes me more active, calm and happy

Actually this art is a science based exercise
That builds up inside of me to get skills wise

Provides me with complete insight into positivity
Ponders me with greater depth of self-creativity

Writing even allows me to communicate emotions
By putting questions answers to explain situations

It gives me pen as tool for applying on my therapy
I flow emotions on to paper with my own ability

I Love Singing

ॐ

I love singing it's an excellent exercise of celebrating oxygen

A priceless way of improving joy ability and sense of rhythm

Sing anyway, lets lungs, heart and mind make you feel relaxed

Hence improve voice, volume, resonance and touch of tune

Actually singing is a way for me to unfurl the sense of pleasure

Music genuinely is the 'food of love' says the great Shakespeare

So I enhance my emotions through singing, choose to play on

And draw my home with music as it's very rare blissful treasure

Singing is a Festival of Joy

૪૭લ્ડ

Singing is a festival of joy, makes balance in breath control
It soothes mind, heart, soul, body, mood and attitude whole
I love singing to capture music and sound of serenity within
Self-prescribed therapy into my life for achieving fitness goal

Inspiring sounds of lyrics heals the heart and abolishes strife
Emotional pattern of beats makes singing a lot more specify
Rhythmic words speak freely everything hidden in thoughts
Ah, that goes in the ears and touch straight to the heart inside

Music is a form of meditation I receive pure divine vibration
Wonderful feeling of music that leads mind and heart as one
Clearly enhances my mental wellbeing and brings a warm glow
I start dancing on music, it's just been polished skill of life fun

Rhythm

I stay close to my favourite activities that makes me feel delight

By singing, dancing, jumping, meditation, I develop my own style

I love working on sewing machine, it's like playing on electric piano

With food boiling cooker vibrations keep making ring we'll know

Make sure writing, knitting, stitching, music rely on rhythm specify

Every day I move with rhythmic tone boost me enough to magnify

Everything on this planet moves with rhythm of music and dances

A continuous rhythm between day-night, summer-winter enhances

With each inhale exhale in and out there is a rhythm in our breathing

Switch over to mind set, feel the melody of inner self is ever singing

Every moment every thought every action is a reflection of rhythm

When sweet rhythm plays music, footsteps moves heart sings within

I feel safe with fun dancing, life laps my toes to my rhythmic beat

Inner voice makes me want to sing, dance each step with my feet

Since we're born, we'll have unique authentic rhythm in heart beat

Be in tune with it, it is a regular perfect symphony of nature wheel

Rhythmical Work

Listen to the sentiments of rhythmical works
With harmonious beauty in language of words

As they are speaking to you in a suitable tone
Emotional beats are patterned in my poem own

Metre is measured by series of sound in verse
Pleasant degree of variation is intertwined in lyrics

A Flow of Emotional Feelings

ಬಿಂಬ

A flow of emotional feelings held in me
With positive negative impact specifically

In a good mood I make the best use of them
I write them in my own sentences effectively

It soothes my body and heals my heart too
I love to write, it's an amazing therapy for me

Words express the sentimental culture of poems
Do you hear the interplay of words rhythmically

Just listen to the sound and voice that tells me
A magical bond of mateship between poem and me

Emotional Mood

ॐ

My emotional mood finds right words to assign
I reveal my feelings on paper and place them in line
For making sound pretty I design in rhythmic rhyme
This is the only way for me to spend my good time

Emotions takes me into a world of sublime peace
I shut myself here my mind feels finally release
The place of peace is a treasure with infinite bliss
No gold no earthly wealth can ever measure this

I want to sing a song of joy in sweet tone of dance
I need to enjoy my own company feel like romance
Now I realize I found my new heavenly home here
It's gift from Heaven stillness surrounds me so dear

The Brand-New Year

සාය

The brand-new year ahead of 365 pages

Let's put words of thoughts on empty pages

The 1st page starts off new year right now

Let's create the life we have imagined always

Keep head always to the sky and feet down low

Let's fill life with virtuous passions and to glow

Pay attention to everything cherish each moment

Let's maintain positivity and move on with own flow

New Year Wish

Sound of midnight Bell tells that year is ending

My heartfelt warm wishes with joy I'm sending

May each new day bring buffet of peace and love

And your goal be accomplished by God's blessings

Dear, focus on your energies that lie inside of you

Just look forward to what comes in front of you

Make sure each day is a God's gift that holds hope

Have a cheerful year ahead I am going to wish you

Tick Tock

Tick tock, tick tock, tick tock, tick tock
My mind is flowing with the time of clock

Few rhythmic lyrics of the ceaseless ticking
All the day long, all the night too ever sticking

Though lyrics of the clock are not too much
But its strong voice keeps alerting farthest

Clock has never got study in rhythmic rhymes
But it ever marks the accurate course of time

Big and small hands afford not a moment of rest
Round-round number to number move with zest

Big hand counts minutes while little counts hour
At the top of 12 both hands together show power

Gentle clock is sticked to the truth in this lie world
Always keeps proper time proudly in its own word

What it speaks day night to itself ever patiently talks
In my hall standing still, from its place never walks

How Time Seems to Fly

How time seems to fly all months gone by
Everyone looks forward to set their goals high
And make their mind with festivals hues bright
I'm writing this poem to say happy new year hi

Each year has its own year in wonderful way
So never miss opportunities of new year day
Be ready for its welcome to celebrate any way
Resolve to change, challenges come your way

New year is a chance for starting up new beginning
A reminder to the sentiment for doing something
Raise your hopes and dreams with mind-set galore
I wish you happy new year with many more blessings

Happy New Year

ॐ

Solemnly clock is moving around number to number
As it strikes 12 in the midnight of 31ˢᵗ December
People all over the world cheer and wish each other
New year is born a bright shiny joyful new year

The year last night is gone, bid the old year Goodbye
Past days race is vanished taken off Swift flight
Another date is stuck in the calendar of our life
Let's celebrate the dates on which we view future life

Happy new year day comes but once in every year
The day is a day of everyone's birthday comes near
Now you grow everyday everyway get better and cheer
Fill your life with blessings towards Happy New Year

The Chapter of Old Year

ಐಡ

The chapter of old year, we are all closing
To welcome new year for its new beginning

Let's pray new year bring back normalcy
So we all may be united with safe feeling

We all had to face difficult time of covid 19
May new year be full of virus free packaging

And that in time the world be a safe place
To a healthy happy lifestyle be it switching

Blissful showers of joy and peace follow us
As the new year brings occasion of celebrating

Brightness

Brightness in the dark I found
Through my meditation profound

Such brightness I ever had seen
Dancing light with golden gleam

Loveliness of my spiritual inner power
So calm so bright I receive a dower

Let me Write

ఠఁౡ

I write my emotions that are quite profound
To keep my words alive the best way I found

Thru writing connection with self keeps me near
Words surround me always whisper in my ear

I make me up inside with the rhythmic worlds
Dance upon my senses, speak to me in poetic words

It keeps my mind lifted makes my world of peace
I am blessed, for it let me write whatever I please

I Don't Have

I don't have any type of academic career
As a poetic art or a creative writer

I just use the balanced words of my feelings
That is a part of my emotional treasure

What is kept in the store of my mind
A hint of secrets of new and old desire

Just through the words in many shapes
I translate the language of my heart insider

It sounds good to me when words capture
The DNA of my thoughts with spark of inspire

It's my way to bring out the clear picture
Of loyalty sincerity and inner pleasure

Copyright

Certainly, this creative art is my moral property
I am the owner of this work with an authority

Creative flow is full of my intensive imagination
As doing work is a passive stance of realization

Circulations of new thoughts are living in my life
Expressions of words are protected by copyright

I am paying attention to pirates who steal words
Upload easily full contents of somebody's works

O' dear, make a priority of getting ideas and facts
Write your experiences in your words with tacts

Respect the copyright who has the right to control
The integrity of work of stuff, the attribution whole

Shopping Mall

ॐ

I embark upon my long trip to the classy mall
An approved energetic medicine for me at all

So I declare that in the hunt for my pleasure
I much more like to turn to across the mall

I head from north to south and east to west
And glance all around shining shopping stall

Noises of number of folks coming going in chaos
Declaring their presence race all over the mall

As I start assessing the outfit of latest styles
I stop looking at faces wandering around mall

I always keep debit card some cash in my purse
With smile on my face shopping from stall to stall

On entering suddenly I notice the label of stuff
Something very special beautiful on store wall

Though my closets are full drawers are spilled
But my unfulfilled heart ever has a great fall

I like to spend money on fabulous classy stuff
Hanging in my closet that matters most of all

my elegant sophisticated style promotes me
Physically mentally fit nourishes me after all

My Dressing Sense

I wear what I want to wear that matters
I dress up for myself not for others

I feel good in my comfortable outfit
It's stylish intellectual and exquisite

I like to wear classy things that suits me
Style defines my attitude my grace in me

My authentic style is a part of my expression
Dressing well is ultimate form of sophistication

My dressing sense depends on the situation
I wear light makeup wherever I am heading

Usually I go for simple, clear clean appearance
It shows my individuality and my confidence

My style speaks about my being who I am
Dress stimulates the sense of unique trend

Two Lives

I have two lives, one half in noisy day bright
Other in silent night, both reveals to my sight

Twinkling stars garnished with celestial moon
Displaying cosmic rays keeping me in tune

The melodious whistling fresh lovely air
I love to move with blooming flowers rare

I come to feel them as two neighbours in simple way
I spend whole day whistling for my bed to lay

Session of Day

Session of day has taken its flight
Stepping swiftly with light feet night

I wonder and confused lost to myself
In day or night where to find myself

Either I need to go in the rising Sun
Or roaming through with Moon begun

I am sinking in the layers of my being
Want to move with mindful breathing

I have to breathe, already in the air
Just wanting to be free for my pleasure

My Wonderful Life

ॐ

My wonderful life is like a movie essentially
I play with self and get experience of reality

Its scrip is concerned with one heroic heart
Directed by the state manager so beautifully

God has given me such good chance to play it
I love my significant role and try to play rightly

By my good karma and with my best effort
I may get an academic award of peace certainly

So 'Suman' will not transform herself in this role
Rather immerse herself in this role harmonically

I Live to Enjoy

ഇൻൽ

I live to enjoy in the class session of my life
By singing, dancing, writing for the joy of inside
Setting priorities and act as heart strongly feels
Doing my best with true intention keeps me alive

Enjoying company of friends having conversation
Getting lost in the world of nature's imagination
Breathing fresh air, watching wind swaying trees
Spending time with family, gaining an appreciation

Feeling of being alive makes my life worth living
I am here right now and days are more fulfilling
Breathing, thinking, doing really matters a lot
I have cause to bless myself in the process of living

I Am Important

ဆာ

I am important to my life and I know my worth
It's important to introduce who I am on this earth

I spend a lot of time with me and shut out the world
I just to let you know how I care myself in the world

Through experience I've learnt one important lesson
I can't please everyone so I dropped off thinking them

Now main priority is mine to make peace within
I've to find the real key of harmony what I have in

Leave behind stress I will focus on my strong setup
More courageous more helpful to get a night sleep well

I will create a rituality of joy and healing as process
And include meditation deep breathing and stillness

I will stretch and exercise for body mind and soul
Represent a brand that will reflect personality whole

Proudly I love being 'Suman' making the best of something
I am writing a chapter, my own self will enjoy reading

Faults

Some people spend time to judge faults in others
While they are colour blind to the faults of theirs

It's very easy to perceive the faults of anyone else
But very crucial looking at the same of our own selves

Actually their eyes don't see themselves clearly
Rather all around they see the eyes of everyone else

Even don't want to take time to look at own selves
Then how can they feel true intention to themselves

If they keep humble sense about faults of own selves
They'll realize enough joy and peace within themselves

To Help Someone

To help some needy by doing something is ever in style
Without any expectation you do it rightly with a smile

Giving the joy to needy people is greater than getting
Spread flavour of love with generosity and forgetting

Little act of love and kindness can be huge to others
Learn from the nature how with love she does nurture

Look how the sunshine comes make our world bright
Sweet fragrance of flowers inspire It's to our heart's delight

Learn from river who carries flow of water for others
River leaves a legacy of love and blessed life forever

Farmer is growing crops to be the food for all humans
Cow gives milk, fruits of tree enjoyed by entire humans

So being a human choose generosity to help someone
Make sure you'll find inner pleasure and peace within

Attitude of Kindness

Attitude of kindness is the richest gem on this sphere
That's the deepest thing inside goes with you everywhere

Show your kindness with smiles it can travel around the earth
When you'll receive smile in return you'll realize it's worth

Kind words about one another represents the joyful gift of life
A gentle soft touch reminds us that human dignity is still alive

This realisation is so kingly so royal raises your head always
Please hold it in your heart and mind and practice it always

Keep spreading your flavour of kindness wherever you go
You will realize your own cup of happiness is ever in flow

Do Your Best

You Try to do your best, God has put you into test
Under any circumstances, ready steady go and get

God has created you to win, Bow to Him with respect
Calmly motivate self, it's a process of trying your best

Time begins from right now, prove it, just take a step
Put your heart into it, that is a leading key of invest

Stand up for your support, make a history beastie best
Practice to win completely, better to go with your gut

Don't decide on judgement, rather you win over or not
But ready to do your best, make it your passion project

Focus on your goal be your own principal capital asset
Tell your story in order to live and love yourself fullest

What Matters the Most

Attraction, richness, talent, education doesn't matter most
The question is how you behave in world, matters the most

In matter of style create pure joy of your inner being
If you share your joy with everyone that matters the most

Joy is a symbol of eternity, it's absolutely a great fact
Invest it in your own abilities that's what matters the most

Find beauty in the littlest things count all that's free
Friendship, family, laughter, love all that matters the most

Usually when I go to my bed in the night, I ask myself
What I have done best today, to me that matter the most

Listen dear, get up, dress up, show up matters not to me
But getting lost in the meaningful research matter the most

I start up with thanks to God gives me passion for writing
Through writing I'm keeping record of what matters the most

Fall in Love

I will fall in love with that someone
Who can well understand my emotion

Read my silence more than my words
Through my eyes and through action

Who can be my support and my hope
And guide me to attain new horizon

Accept me even with my all mistakes
Love me with heart and soul someone

Miss me and want me to be with him
I will fall in love with a such genuine

Who can forgive me after an argument
Certainly on him, I will shower blossom

Wear Smile

On my face I always wear a warm smile
Joy in my shining eyes is my own style

It's my most fashionable effective way
To hide thousands of hurts deep inside

But nobody takes the time to find out
What lies hidden behind blissful smile

I cry behind the close doors bitterly
And come out, say Hello with smile

Even my known can't judge my face
How I fight with the battle of my life

If someone is sure he knows me well
But he knows not my silent pain I hide

Smile is a trigger of my inner strength
Social gatherings keep my sparkle alive

My smiling attitude is to save my face
No matter whatever's happening inside

I want to enjoy my life before it's over
Make it a heaven and live for my life

So I wear smile that complete my beauty
The most expensive ornament of all time

No Person Has the Right

No person has the right to hurt me internally
Soft corner of my heart no one can ever see

Heavy heart cries silently with dropping tears
Tensing body turns completely shocked with fear

So I push such people to get lost from my world
Because they hurt my emotions by their words

I do not want to live my life always worrying
Having fun rather than in self-pity wallowing

I'll fill my aching heart with my inner strength
And reflect how can I heal heart by my sentiments

I'll go ahead with my little privacy and maintain it
Without expecting to receive any formal credit

I am sharing my disturbed feelings on paper
A burden is lifted off makes me feel better

God Stands

ഈരു

God stands at our door ever
As the greatest cheerful giver
So sweet is the will of the Lord
With His full hands He gives ever

He gives and gives in abundance
More than our needs whatsoever
He is able to make all grace abound
To enhance the serenity of pleasure

Leave all in His hands and embraces
Find true joy in everything forever
Come let's sing our songs of praise
For His royal love endures forever

Myself

Hey, it's me, I am in love only with myself
I enjoy my company to take care of myself
I am fully aware, that is why I am very rare
Inner voice which says the reality of myself

I don't want to be fit in any someone's life
I am happy within the little world of myself
I am for myself, talk to self and listen to me
I keep getting with this belief in loving myself

Values of self-respect is my foremost priority
No can handle me the way just I carry myself
I am the director and actor of my life actions
And fully confident to produce story of myself

Creative skill makes me feel working nonstop

I get stuck particular on the dialogue of myself

I like to spend my valuable time with me alone

Heart's song, mind's dance, I celebrate myself

I, this entire Universe, I am more than enough

I need not appropriate approval about myself

long life romance with self is awesome feeling

I am the romantic person in the world of myself

I am never alone, I have me, l and my own self

Love me or hate, I am still gonna shine in myself

My personality speaks the language of my spirit

My style reflects my ability and attitude of myself

It's Me vs Me

ೞೞ

Hey, it's me vs me and always been just me
I live in my own little world that's ok with me

God has entrusted me on this planet with myself
I enjoy life to the fullest that wants to live in me

I don't want to live show off life to impress others
I've made my choices in my way and always will be

I've many problems in my life but have solution also
I just have a stronger sense about me to protect me

Having contact with me makes my private life active
I've found the meaning of life by living alone with me

I've got a gift of rhymes by the Divine Grace of God
  I hold all close to my heart that's mean a lot to me

  I see glimpses of beauty in my soul, I hint by write
  As for as words can give a view of sound within me

  I see myself sensitive skilful tie my wrist with words
  I Pen down and write out usual occurrence with me

  I'm my only competitor not competing with any one
  I'm the master of my mind my thoughts to my life key

I simply follow my intensive feelings of my own reality
And work on myself competitively on me by me far me

My goal of life is to do best, try to pursue certain types
My life is defined by my plans by my trials only by me

I like to keep private myself, no interference of anyone
I simply do what I do in my life, no one can do for me

I try to get myself grounded and prefer to be true self
I stay on my side and be an advocate in favour of me

I put myself first because I'll spending rest of life with
My life is really only mine so I like romance with me

who I'm in love with, I wanna let you know right now
You have to keep an eye on the title of 'it's me vs me'

Reminder to Me

Some time I need a little push to remind me for me

How feeling of overwhelmed wonderful life can be

For inner peace do everything in a calm quite spirit

I tell myself, inhale hold exhale and breathe deeply

Now relax, good or bad or hard things what so ever

Happenings in my surroundings are just temporarily

So dear embrace each moment God gives is precious

With singing dancing writing techniques create ability

Eat healthy good food, wear fancy clothes that matter

Enjoy it of course in order to live extraordinary joyfully

I have little bit of passion to do the best in all situation

Truly that inspiration comes by meditation profoundly

God pours ideas in to my attitude to write my poems

The light of His abundant blessings falling down on me

I am fully satisfied with what I have, is a peaceful mind

I am enriched and aware in every way to survive really

Relation

Let us focus on connection with our great relation
Let go their mistakes, fling ourselves into affiliation
Mistakes are the single chapter in a part of our life
But relations are the complete book of association

So turn and turn page to know something specific
The real magical pages are the perfect replication
It's very important to read each page of the book
And get along with colourful pages of all relation

Stream of Tears

৪০০৪

Stream of tears from unblinking eyes that makes me weep so
Don't wipe tears off my cheeks, let tempest of sighs blow

My tongue is silent but tears are the language of my eyes
They carry heavy feelings of my all pain, joy and sorrow

Through life, I've learnt to hide bleed within my heart
And to conceal facts about the matter that hurts me so

Truly I laugh in strength but broken heart bleeds tears
I wipe it away by tears while laughing attitude show

I greet myself in a way with tears and poem in eyes
My tears are closest to me, it's okay to let them flow

Mission of Finding

୫୦୨

I am lost to myself and struggling to find me
Who I am, where I am, what's going on with me

Well, though everything else is found on Google
But tell me, where to find a person of inside me

On the outside of my appearance what I show
In fact that one is not real, I'm at war with me

I ask myself what for I am in this eternal world
What's my aim, not knowing where I stand to be

Searching for my true self just can't seem to find
But my mission of finding is still continued to be

I do not give up moving just around and around
I'm the centre of my world, it means a lot to me

Here I must tell you the process of my emotions
I love me so much and feel elated to be loved by me

Once I may find my significant self, I'll never let go
I can be myself only when I'll bring back the real me

I convince me with a smile, I must show me the way
Mission of finding will be accomplished only by me

Don't Cry for Me

ॐ

Don't be surprised if someday I will not wake
My breathing will stop, my soul God will take

Don't cry for me as it was just my time to go
I was not meant to stay here, someday I'd to go

We're all mortal beings, born alone, die alone
In spite of company, with life we all fight alone

Accept the ultimate truth of life, death is confirm
When where takes us in to a country of no return

You'll probably be shocked on this saddest part
Don't cry for me as my peaceful soul is on rest

So let it be welcome, release me just with similes
Hero is going home, just know I've made rhymes

It's begin of eternal journey going home to God
Sing mantras at my funeral my soul is in the mood

Fire in Principles

ℬꙄ

If you've fire in principles then it's necessary to collide
If you're alive then it's necessary for you to appear alive

You must have seen hard time in subduing of true fact
And at the point of fire in principles you are living yet

You collide with convincing arguments standing on ground
In your own way you choose the fairness in right and wrong

No doubt your mind is enriched with powerful concepts
That's why you need to share crashes of real life's targets

Your passion is burning inside of you with focus strong
Deep principles moral values records how you lived life long

What matters most is you saw your personal integrity
Your life is a result of life's principles a degree of authenticity

Sunny Morning

In the era of sunny morning Sun hits my face
My eyes are dazzled by the bright Sun's rays
I struggle to open eyes stretch my rested body
As I get lovely soothing sparkling sunny waves

Oh' wonderful radiant light glaring around me
So rich fully brightened twinkling with glee
I feel alive first seeing of sunny waves dance
Sun staggers with pouring golden glory to me

I'm expressing the essence of inner joy in words
Writing on my page with smart rhythmic colours
I'm feeling the choreography of dancing sun rays
The melody of bright air is smiling in my world

Every Sunrise

Every Sunrise is a wave of new beginning
A new era in life comes in a new rhythm
Don't take it for granted, get value for it
Because it arises with most precious fiction

The sun sees a new born day with new eyes
Greet the lavish sun shine, salute with smiles
Now you are stepping from night to morning
Unfurl yourself with great joy and blessed life

It's time for spreading wings of hope and fly
Leave the era gone behind and say goodbye
Adorn your mind, heart and body with love
Embrace the challenges and hold your head high

Newness of the day encourages to do amazing

You're given a second chance for new beginning

It's an opportunity to enjoy the journey of life

Breathe freely, be grateful, be glad you're living

Now My Life

I faced so many good and bad ways in my life
But never get down; pour myself in every strife

Now I have crossed the struggling part of my life
I made it easy by having courage and faith inside

Now I am fully aware that life goes on with flow
Let me go with the flow and lit up in golden glow

Now my life is filled with peace and contentment
I live love my life fullest and enjoy every moment

Also I keep connection with the senior section
And give cheer to my life and love to everyone

Now I love to sing lyrics in my praise with pride
And happily I am going to give myself a big five

Now I am writing on page about my elegant life
At least it will always remain hidden in the file

Aging Process

I am dealing with dusty growing age of old
It's a natural process of years playing role

I accept this passage of years gracefully
But refuse to accept natural order absolutely

Though my body is not strong like it used to be
But still I am the same being as I used to be

So I don't allow aging process bring me down
When I still have value and ability to move on

God has sent me for a purposeful mission
To live love with kind heart is His commission

I always swim in the joy of spiritual flow
I have my original self-having inside glow

Don't study my face, my eyesight is fine
Hair turned black to grey is the fashion of time

Age is a ladder of numbers, my mind stays young
How lucky I am with sound health flowering

Staying Young

Not anyone can stay young forever
We are all destined to grow older

Though we've to climb ladder of number
But let my cheerful mind stay younger

When my body feels healthy and sound
And I can move still around and around

Strength of my voice can call out loud
My straight shoulder, my spine my proud

My teeth are still strong and still bright
Even I do yoga, meditation keeps me alive

Well, well even I have got still fine ear
What is going on around me I can hear

Hence I am flexible and easily can dance
On the sounding floor swift lights glance

I still write poetry of sorrows and joys
I sing lyrics full throat, you can hear guys

Well versed my own rhymes I love to sing
Like the harmonious sphere that bring

So dear this thing of old age is not for me
I have got concession and perception free

My heart is still shimmering like gold
Nothing is wrong with me still am bold

So please don't stare at me in this way
I am staying young, ain't that okay

I am shown here in my every word
Creative mind makes my mark in this world

My Little Universe

৪০০৪

Poetry is my little universe, in it I make my own world
At last, here I find myself take playful rhythmic words

In fact it's all my mind matter directly subjected to me
Happening in my life and surrounding I write usually

I am one of many who writes rhythmic poetry everyday
It seems like a game so I love doing writing for to play

I just let my words maintain discipline to make a sound
String them together so they may express as best on ground

I shape them, mould them as I play with solemn words
In this lonely ground, words are everything my world

Some people say, writing is a waste of time without pay
But I play for my pleasure it's all that I need to win day

I Am in Love

Oh' I am in love with writing rhythmic rhyme
This literary attitude of mine is always in prime

Writing spirit comes from my musical education
So there is a musical imperative in my sensation

In my choice I look for rhythm and tone in verse
Almost in classic style of rhythmic beauty in words

The words of my heart hints at the story to come
The main layers of my emotions come to action

Rhyming words with sentences set a beautiful poem
Interplay of my feelings evoke metres and rhythm

I keep rhyming and post them into an internet site
Without any literary fame or reward or pay I do write

It's an enjoyable hobby to me, in truth I can say
It brings inner joy for me, too hard to give away

I write rhymes because there's a voice within me
I feel Ooh it's my love of rhymes speak love for me

Dignity

෴

To live with dignity lifestyle is an art
I have built it with my own good thought

Leaving all ups and downs of life behind
I sketch human realization in my mind

I paint selfless sentiments in my heart
Loyally mark this special work as an art

I shape regard and affection in my embrace
And keep it dearly in my special place

I carve human dignity that's open for all
Trace true work on love that links with all

Separated all my ego from the painted scene
I've freed myself from all as dignified being

    INWARD REFLECTIONS

Special Contribution from my Grandson Gurvaansh Vasu Khosla. He wrote these poems, when he was 10 years of age

Football

ఐరా

Football is our proud

it unites us all

We should get backup

whenever we fall

Life is our test

you gotta give your best

It's already written on your fate

you can do anything mate

With hard work and dedication

you'll outplay them all

Success does not come early

it always comes after a fall

You'll be an inspiration in the Hall of Fame

Everyone with respect, will take your name

One day you'll see the moon and its craters

And shut the mouth of your haters and traitors

Prayer

It's a prayer of Neolithic age
expressing the hopes and fears in their stage

We bow down to you 'O Sun'
We hope that you keep giving us
Brightness warmth tons and tons

We worship you, 'O Mother Earth'
You are our sacred place of birth

'O Stars', you show us the right direction
We play to you with full allegiance and devotion

We are thankful to you 'O Water and Rain'
Without you we can't grow crops and grain

We hope that you help fulfilling our needs and desires
We are all blessed by your supreme divinity entire

We pray to you, 'O Mighty Thunder'
For us you are an unexpected wonder

You provide us a bounty 'O Sacred Cow'
We are grateful to you and before you, we all bow

You have frightened us, 'O Furious Snake'
Your deadly fear has put our lives on stake

QUOTES

Life is a treasure only when we make each day useful &
pleasant and enjoy sharing it with each other

৪০৫৪

What we do practically every time in perfect way, matters
the most.

৪০৫৪

You never know which second is going to be your last, so do
what you love.

৪০৫৪

Give your hands to serve and open your hearts to love as
long as you can, as wide as you can for others, especially for
yourself.

৪০৫৪

I salute the Indian Army for their unwavering dedication, courage,
sacrifice and commitment and feel proud to be an Indian.

৪০৫৪

What we do practically in perfect way to others that defines
our attitude, our personality and our image.

৪০৫৪

If we want a chamber in Heaven, we have to make Heaven
in our mind and heart.

ॐ

We should understand the true value of present moment and
enjoy our life and be Happy. It's all that matters.

ॐ

Life is a bitter truth. Yes, it is! Accept this reality. Grow
good ideas in the garden of your mind. Take action to be
victorious. A better life awaits you.

ॐ

A faith with God is the most important connection. God is
just like Wi-Fi, every time online. We simply can connect
with Him every day through the correct password 'Faith'.

ॐ

A girl is the blessed Angel of God. After marriage she
enters her husband's home and carries with her the blissful
attitude of lifelong commitment and puts the colours of
tenderness, happiness and patience inside her husband's
world. So, realise her value and give her full respect.

ॐ

Dear Gentlemen! Never ever think that after marriage wife is your property. Give respect and get respect is the only law of life. Remember! A woman has her own personality, own individuality, own identification that grows according to her own idealism.

෨෬

Little moments shared with her man matters most to a woman.

෨෬

Focus on becoming the right person first, and then stand strong. Achieving the goal of being the right person, in the right place, at the right time, has the power to captivate anyone's heart.

෨෬

A woman's enthusiastic spirit is the most significant blessing to mankind. No creation is possible without woman. She is the symbol of care, share, kindness, love, grace and dignity.

෨෬

A Mother serves as a source of positive inspiration, radiating brilliance and humility. She is a role model for her child, fostering an environment filled with joy, love, and peace.

෨෬

Dear Gentlemen! If you expect an angel woman in your life, firstly, you have to bring heaven for her on this earth.

୫୬

Teach your children to understand the ultimate values of life by your own richer experiences.

୫୬

What you do for your children in an attempt to satisfy their all demands is not enough. Important is how you guide them in the cultivation of the right attitude towards life.

୫୬

Abundant luxury is the enemy for the mental and physical growth of a child. If the child is given everything he wants, he will never learn the value of money and time. So, create a healthy balance for your child.

୫୬

Parents need to give such type of guidelines to their children that will help them to develop skills and responsibilities with self-confidence. Such types of habits are transmitted from one generation to the next.

୫୬

Children should learn at an early age that what they get is
earned with big efforts of someone's hard work. So, they
have to merit what they receive in the world and understand
the value of everything.

☙❧

Children are the future. Be their companion with open
heart and mind to understand their feelings and ideas.
Support them, Protect them, Encourage them, so that they
may be able to know the value of Self Esteem and grow
in the understanding of Love, Affection, Respect and
Blessings.

☙❧

Dear Parents! Strive to be an exemplary role model for your
children, inspiring them to thrive with positivity in a world
full of challenges. Lead by demonstrating your virtuous
qualities, rather than simply instructing them on what to do.
In time, they will grow up, reflect on the way you treated
them, and embody the kind of true, compassionate human
beings you nurtured them to be.

☙❧

Children are like delicate flowers, thriving in the warmth of
love, kindness, and care. As elders, it is our responsibility
to guide and nurture them with compassion. We should also
openly acknowledge and praise their qualities, both in front

of others and in private, so they develop a strong sense of self-worth and confidence.

৪৩

Dear Parents! Remember, today you're keeping your children closer to you. Tomorrow your children will keep you closer to them. How sweet and magical the Space of Time is. Today's children will tomorrow become the parents to their parents.

৪৩

We ordinarily rely upon materialistic values to enjoy life in wearing branded clothes to glorify our beauty and status but we forget that everything changes with the time. Live intensely and have genuine connection with the people whom you love and respect.

৪৩

Never focus on your obstacles and complain to God, Oh God, I've big obstacles. Always try to say, Oh obstacles, I've big God. All problems will be blown away.

৪৩

God is great. What He can do nobody can. He always has good plans for us better than anything others could offer.

৪৩

When burning desire for God lights up in the soul, heart becomes the Temple of God and God comes running to dwell within. The seeker who wants his home in Heaven, by the Grace of God, is granted Heaven in his own heart.

ॐ

I cherish the constant gift of God's presence and find joy in walking amidst the beauty of nature.

ॐ

Life is a temporary phase of passing clouds, so don't dwell on it—just keep moving forward. From my perspective, the key to positive change in life lies in changing your mindset. That's what truly makes a difference.

ॐ

We all come to this world in the same way. But leave this world in a different way.

ॐ

A pulsating desire for love is the most powerful missile on this planet.

ॐ

You can't mean 'I Love You' in three words. It carries a profound meaning of a devoted heart. I Bow Down to Love Supreme.

৪৩

Flirt with your understanding of joyous moments. Romance with true pleasures. Get engaged with the blooms of free spirit and marry the liberty of generosity. Divorce egoism, love yourself. That matters in life.

৪৩

In the garden of my heart, there is always a quiet, sacred space where my thoughts, actions, and words are devoted to God. He is both my teacher and my inspiration. I delight in praising Him with the instrument of my mind, singing songs of faith and glory to Him.

৪৩

Acknowledge your own self-worth and honour your own heart feelings.

৪৩

When you say 'No,' it simply means 'Not now.' Every 'No' establishes a boundary for your faith and self-respect. Therefore, remain strong and hold on just a bit longer.

৪৩

Good heart sees goodness everywhere.

಄ഽ಄

Simplicity is a graceful majestic style of sophistication.

಄ഽ಄

Dignity is paramount for an honourable person.

಄ഽ಄

Real respect comes from within, from the quiet thoughts of
a humble heart.

಄ഽ಄

I like being on my own and want people to like me as I am.

಄ഽ಄

I'm not trying to be better than anyone else. I'm just trying
to beat my own best.

಄ഽ಄

Dignity is a symbol of Identity and of Integrity.

಄ഽ಄

God has put the desire for some particular work in every
heart and mind.

ॐ

Immerse yourself in work that matters to you, giving it your
all and dedicating yourself fully.

ॐ

Creative people are the luckiest on this planet. They do
what they imagine with more faith and find a way to express
it to the entire world.

ॐ

Our creative thoughts and actions manifest the result we
desire.

ॐ

In my opinion work of art is the mirror of our own life,
in which our creativity is reflected. We all fill our life in
beautiful colours of patience, peace and love with our skilful
abilities.

ॐ

When you've passion and inspiration for work, you'll always
go right.

ॐ

Look inside yourself, embrace your true self and enjoy the
simple joys of life.

୫୬

Living peacefully on this glorious planet is like enjoying
stillness in all circumstances and calmness in soul.

୫୬

Silent prayer is the majestic gateway to God's Kingdom,
the path to the Divine. Those who understand this are
graced with the light of God's favour.

୫୬

Peace is ever present within us. But we neutralize the peace
with disturbing thoughts and restlessness. That's why peace
is elusive.

୫୬

Why seek peace outside, when it originates from inside.

୫୬

Nobody can bring you peace, but only you.

୫୬

Learn to appreciate silence. Its sweetest essence flows like melodies through the halls of God's infinite mansion.

଼

Cling to the consciousness of peace that is above all earthly dignities.

଼

Peaceful mind can establish supreme peace on earth.

଼

When you look within and see God as your hero, and when you recognize God in everyone around you, you become a hero of God.

଼

Calm your inner warrior. God is in control.

଼

O' my God, you are my world and my world is yours. Without you, there is no world.

଼

Immerse your mind in the power of prayer, allowing it to become a source of strength, peace, and clarity. Through prayer, you tap into a profound energy that nurtures your spirit, guiding your thoughts and actions with purpose and faith.

ഓരു

Doing good and feeling good is the essence of true faith.

ഓരു

Respond wisely to unpleasantness by activating your inner strength. The power of your inner spark is within you, enabling you to rise above any situation and manage your life's circumstances with calmness and perfect tranquillity.

ഓരു

Turn your mind on to the healing powers of God's grace.

ഓരു

We are all placed on this earth to do good for others in every way, at all times and in every place. Embracing humility through acts of kindness is the essence of true happiness.

ഓരു

When inner achievement is attained, it brings about a profound shift in external realities, filling our lives with greater joy and enduring peace.

ॐ

To transform the world into a happier, more peaceful place, the change must first begin within the hearts of each of us who inhabit this planet.

ॐ

Instead of doing it then, do it right now.

ॐ

If you know how to find it, you'll always have time for anything.

ॐ

Live your life to impress yourself rather than to flatter others.

ॐ

Live the life you love to imagine

ॐ

Our positivity shapes and reflects our true identity.

ॐ

Let your moral consciousness be your guide.

෫෬

When you do something kind for someone, you'll also
experience a deep sense of joy within yourself.

෫෬

Hardened hearts often respond with violence, hatred,
and destruction. The only way to end this cycle of misery
is through LOVE. Guide them away from the path of
violence and towards the call of peace, joy, and harmony.

෫෬

Always believe, a miracle is on the cards for you.

෫෬

No matter what your age is, keep aspiring higher.

෫෬

Don't simply count the years of your age; let each year be
filled with vibrant, meaningful days that truly matter.

෫෬

Life can be full of challenges, but we must navigate it wisely and find clever, effective solutions that turn even the toughest situations into opportunities for growth and success.

ೞೞ

My life is determined with my own rules. I've my own attitude towards my God, towards my life, towards my duties to enjoy every single moment of life.

ೞೞ

I act on what I think. I express what I feel. I stand by what I say, and my words reflect my personal integrity.

ೞೞ

A winning mindset embraces a remarkable lifestyle.

ೞೞ

Living in peace is the most beautiful way of life.

ೞೞ

The mind, will, and energy are the true pillars of the body, providing essential stability for natural balance and a harmonious lifestyle.

ೞೞ

I like being alone freely by giving full attention to loving silence. It's my way to restore energy and to connect with inner light of soul to heal mentally and physically.

ॐ

Self-realization transforms us by shedding our old, desire-driven personality and replacing it with a renewed self, purified by the enlightening rays of priceless knowledge.

ॐ

Mutual respect is the key ingredient that defines and sustains healthy, thriving relationships.

ॐ

Every relationship is built on trust, patience, understanding, honesty, respect, and communication. It is a journey of self-discovery and a shared expression of emotions.

ॐ

Faith truly becomes faith through the act of obedience.

ॐ

Place genuine faith in God, and you'll naturally feel better.

ॐ

Belief in God shines forth as light, and light reflects God's presence.

ॐ

Tune your mental radio with the pure divine harmony and enjoy the cosmic vibration that invokes the presence of God within.

ॐ

Obedience is the highest testament to our trust in God.

ॐ

The power of faith & hope in God can scatter light all over and one single virtuous soul can eliminate all evils of hatred by one mission of love.

ॐ

The essence of God's law is summed up in one word: Love.

ॐ

As you draw nearer to divine love through your heart and self-sacrifice, you may find yourself in constant communion with God, a connection that guides you daily.

ॐ

Embrace the understanding that we are creations of God, each holding true love within. Therefore, we must respect and love all people, filling the world with love.

৯০৫৪

Love exists solely to express love.

৯০৫৪

Love is intrinsic to our nature; it clings to us as we cling to it.

৯০৫৪

True love is in union with the beloved God.

৯০৫৪

In moments of silence, your soul begins to communicate with you.

৯০৫৪

Faith is my lifeline.

৯০৫৪

Continuously keeping God in your thoughts is the path to pleasing Him.

৯০৫৪

Meditation is the key for connecting deeply with God.

෨ॐ

Dedicate ample time to silence and meditation both morning and evening to recharge your mental energy.

෨ॐ

A strong sense of devotion enriches the quality of our lives.

෨ॐ

A person with strong faith is grounded in both practicality and spirituality.

෨ॐ

Hear God's message during meditation.

෨ॐ

All our actions are being done by God through us.

෨ॐ

Listen attentively and comprehend others before speaking, and you'll become an effective communicator.

෨ॐ

How you handle life and interact with your environment defines your personality and attitude.

૭૭૦૪

The warmth of our persistent smiles can inspire countless people to confront their fears and overcome their troubles.

૭૭૦૪

Everything looks bright just behind a sincere smile.

૭૭૦૪

Never interpret my silence as weakness; it is the loudest expression of my strength and wisdom.

૭૭૦૪

Maintain a sharp and resilient mind.

૭૭૦૪

The present moment is full of meaning.

૭૭૦૪

God has a plan for your life that exceeds your wildest dreams.

૭૭૦૪

Prioritize your spiritual life, and God will ease all other
aspects of it.

৪০৫৪

When you are going through tough times, don't be
discouraged. Pray to God and you never know when His
blessings will move in your favour.

৪০৫৪

God doesn't ask us to fill our lives with countless events or
to seek approval from others, but rather to love one another.

৪০৫৪

A woman in her essence is a divine gift to the world. Her
natural disposition of mind, heart and soul embodies love,
gentleness and a passion that transcends imagination.

৪০৫৪

A woman, God's most loving creation, can embrace all emotions
at once and becomes stronger through prayers and hope.

৪০৫৪

An empowered woman exudes confidence and
determination, rising in her unique, heroic way, inspiring
others to live boldly and vibrantly.

৪০৫৪

God gave us eyes, mouths, hands, and ears, each with its purpose. So, use them wisely.

ॐ

Love and embrace yourself, for it will illuminate your life beautifully.

ॐ

Do not underestimate the power of a woman. She lives with boldness and passion, drawing strength from her unique mindset.

ॐ

Love may be a small word, but its meaning runs deep. Saying "I love you" is easy, but its true significance is complex.

ॐ

Love between two people is like a harmonious dance between champions.

ॐ

Life is beautiful, so let's colour it with patience, understanding, confidence, and brilliant ideas.

ॐ

To be truly kind, open your arms to embrace love, letting warmth fill your heart.

හ෴ශ

A woman is the glue that binds her family, and her love endures forever.

හ෴ශ

A true gentleman understands the futility of unnecessary arguments and wisely opts for silence instead.

හ෴ශ

A gentleman does everything what she wants, while a woman does as she pleases.

හ෴ශ

Love is caring for one another, even in anger.

හ෴ශ

Determined mind with sincere efforts can achieve any goal.

හ෴ශ

Inhale God Exhale God. I cherish this feeling my dear God.

හ෴ශ

When facing an opponent, defeat him with the miraculous
power of love.

෨෫

In this chaotic world, we should adopt the art of meditation,
which is a gateway to divine grace. Hear God's voice
within.

෨෫

Embark on the spiritual journey to divine light, a path filled
with true joy. The journey lies within your heart, where
precious gems adorn the soul in radiant light.

෨෫

Be an angel to others through virtuous deeds, finding joy
within yourself. Help, kind words, gratitude with a smile
and expecting nothing in return: that's the highest form of
angelic assistance.

෨෫

Noble qualities aren't reserved for saints and sages alone.
Anyone can experience the joy of God through meditation
and noble deeds.

෨෫

O God, fill my heart with love, compassion and understanding, so that I may embrace everyone with humanity.

෨෬

Humility is the ultimate expression of love, a powerful and enriching attitude that can holistically heal the world.

෨෬

A spiritual life is one of deep intimacy and love with God—so close, sacred, and peaceful. I live mindfully, blossoming into my true self. O dear God, may this joy always be with me.

෨෬

Spirituality is not a passing trend; it's my lifestyle of mindfulness, enabling me to live harmoniously in a big rhythmic way.

෨෬

Through meditation, I refine my breathing, which in turn enhances my outward appearance.

෨෬

The secrets of God's inner beauty are gifts freely given to those who experience deep communion with Him.

෨෬

Living a spiritual life is an uplifting journey, granting an irrevocable gift of love with self.

౸౹

I am a beautiful creation of God and He makes no mistakes. So, I am beautiful in my own unique way and none can bring me down.

౸౹

Original: I invoke towards me the consciousness of a Queen. The highest degree of my attitude is to observe myself without any judgement.

౸౹

Inner beauty naturally guides one towards spirituality. Satyam Shivam Sundaram (Truth, Godliness, Beauty).

౸౹

Purity within the heart is much more important than outer layers of beauty.

౸౹

For radiant, glowing skin, cultivate good habits and thoughts, letting your inner light shine through.

౸౹

My personal style is unique. I don't dress up according to fashion but I am fashionable in my own way. My fashion is comfortable and elegant, reflecting the essence of who I am.

෴

I always carry a warm smile and joy in my eyes, even when concealing countless pains. I relish life's journey, and a smile is the finest adornment of my inner harmony.

෴

My actions speak for my graciousness, and I no longer feel the need to prove myself to others.

෴

Spirituality unites us with the divine.

෴

My dear, live life with a touch of sparkle.

෴

I keep my heart youthful and full of charm, guided by love and prayer in every moment. I spread joy and kindness wherever I go, triumphing over the passage of time. This is my spiritual way of living.

෴

My approach to aging draws strength from within, allowing
me to live in balanced harmony. As I grow older, I channel
my creativity with increasing skill, and the simplicity of my
life brings mental and physical grace. I present myself with
confidence in every encounter, undeniable by all.

☙❧

Purity within the heart is much more important than outer
layers of beauty.

☙❧

If your thoughts are lively but your mind is steady, you
possess an irresistible charisma.

☙❧

The eyes silently reveal the story of a person's life.

☙❧

When I look in the mirror, I tell myself I love who I am,
striving only to surpass my own standards.

☙❧

Our eyes, the priceless gift, allow us to fully appreciate the
beauty of the world.

☙❧

I am okay being me. I don't need anyone's approval.

ॐ

I serve as a beautiful reminder of life's wonderful moments.

ॐ

I will always remain loyal to you as long as you are steady in
your loyalty.

ॐ

Take time for yourself and explore new places to rekindle
your inner radiance.

ॐ

I have God's love every time with me. I don't need anything
else.

ॐ

True happiness is found in living each moment with
love, grace, and gratitude. Don't blame God for your
challenges—change yourself to find peace and harmony.

ॐ

Happiness is a state of mind and emotion, characterized by
deep inner joy and contentment.

ॐ

Being in love transforms everything. Love alters our thoughts and reshapes our world, healing even the deepest emotional wounds. So, keep loving.

☙❧

Life's meaning isn't found in merely breathing, but in dedicating yourself to loving others and creating something with purpose.

☙❧

If we align our thoughts with the greatness of God, His grace will always be with us.

☙❧

All human beings have incredible abilities within; allow yourself to discover them.

☙❧

Mind is mighty power, but it must be trained to focus on uplifting thoughts.

☙❧

Don't dwell on the past, start anew. If we keep moving forward, new paths will open, leading us to our goals.

☙❧

The mind is like a king. You must rule over it, rather than
let it rule over you.

෪෭

Trust yourself to tackle the stress that life brings your way.

෪෭

When my mind aligns with my vision, my heart believes,
and my soul attains a heavenly state of fulfilment.

෪෭

Do not fear anything, let fear itself be what you challenge.
This is God's reminder to live fearlessly.

෪෭

Don't worry about how others view your weaknesses or
limitations. God doesn't focus on those. He values your
willingness. Trust in Him, and He will enhance your
abilities, both spiritually and practically.

෪෭

Let's discover a serene place of inner joy and immerse
ourselves in spiritual awakening. Release the worries and let
go of the fears that trouble us.

෪෭

Let go of your worries. Stop overthinking, relax, and allow yourself to soar freely.

৯০৪

No one can assist someone indefinitely unless they make an effort to help themselves.

৯০৪

Your idea won't come to life until you make efforts to bring it into action.

৯০৪

Love is founded on mutual understanding, expressed through heartfelt gestures of affection, peace, respect, and togetherness.

৯০৪

The true essence of emotions lies in kind gestures of affection and goodwill.

৯০৪

God's love is always surrounding us like a gentle breeze. We just need to open our hearts to receive its abundance.

৯০৪

Dedicate a meaningful portion of your time to silence and
meditation.

80CR

Carry yourself like a queen on this earth, without worrying
about who else may hold the title around you.

80CR

My graceful and radiant attitude is God's greatest gift to
me, and it defines who I truly am.

80CR

If you have feelings for me, speak up. Otherwise, turn away,
don't take me for granted.

80CR

Cultivate the right mindset by focusing on what matters
most, and appreciate the beauty that surrounds you.

80CR

Elegance is a refined expression of precision, a graceful
demeanour that truly captures one's essence.

80CR

Dignity is of utmost importance for a honourable person.

80CR

Each person is a reflection of their background and experiences.

ഔ

I am a reflection of God, and His blessings are upon me every second, minute, and hour.

ഔ

I must dedicate myself to choosing what truly matters, and commit to living in divine consciousness as my guiding principle.

ഔ

The entire universe serves as God's grand laboratory.

ഔ

God infuses His soul into the world through human thought, and people form their living connections through their decisions, intelligence, and experiences.

ഔ

Cultivate a positive attitude toward those around you, and by doing so, share your optimistic outlook on life.

ഔ

Live life fearlessly, take risks, and stay prepared for
whatever comes next.

℘℘

Don't approach life as if it's merely about existing.

℘℘

Lead a simple and balanced life, as the universe itself
follows simple laws.

℘℘

A life of simplicity and elevated thought is a guaranteed
path to happiness.

℘℘

To be happy is very simple but to be simple is not that simple.

℘℘

Be certain, my dear, that self-improvement is one of the
greatest investments you can make in yourself.

℘℘

Reflect on your true motives. The art of thinking for, with,
and by yourself will shape everything else in your life.

℘℘

Beautiful things happen only when you make a distance
from negativity and pointless dramas.

ಬಾ

The original fragrance of pleasure and joyous moments are
forever sweet memories to remember, never withering never
fading.

ಬಾ

Finding happiness with what you have in the "laboratory"
of your life is a reflection of living in harmony.

ಬಾ

Look within, embrace who you are, and dance in the simple
joy of life.

ಬಾ

The essence of living well is found in joyfully engaging with
others and life's activities.

ಬಾ

For ages, we have aligned our lives with the rhythm of the
cosmos.

ಬಾ

An awakened soul finds the most intimate love within their own personal universe.

૭୦୯ଷ

Stay mindful always. Love yourself. Begin by transforming yourself before helping others.

૭୦୯ଷ

Immerse yourself in purposeful work with passion and dedication.

૭୦୯ଷ

Always give your best effort in life, and then unwind in your own unique way.

૭୦୯ଷ

When your work is driven by passion and inspiration, you'll always be on the right path.

૭୦୯ଷ

No one hurts us. It's our expectations that do.

૭୦୯ଷ

With an open mind and laughter, I make others feel at ease, as I don't let anything get in the way of my happiness.

૭୦୯ଷ

The fulfilment of doing a good job turns you into a master
of wisdom.

ॐ

Simplicity is a graceful and majestic form of elegance.

ॐ

Inner joy is nourishment for the soul.

ॐ

The very essence of unrestrained joyful emotions blossom
from within.

ॐ

God is truly great. What He can accomplish is unmatched,
and His plans for us are always better than anyone else's.

ॐ

Trust in God, for He is always watching over you.

ॐ

God is the real jewel of the heart.

ॐ

Those who trust in God's joy are adorned with a string of
pearls, woven with His love and grace.

৪৩

Tune in to your heart and hear its rhythmic melody; soon,
your feet will dance like never before.

৪৩

Without being swayed by others, follow the path of your heart.

৪৩

We are the creatures of our own reality.

৪৩

Those who see evil in others often harbour the same roots of
evil within themselves.

৪৩

A person with a beautiful heart brings kindness with them
wherever they go.

৪৩

Pain doesn't always signify injury, just as symptoms don't
always indicate illness.

৪৩

When the heart is full of radiant love, the flame of love will continually illuminate the soul.

৪৩

Cultivate a large heart to comprehend even the smallest minds.

৪৩

Nurture your heart with uplifting thoughts and the joy of simplicity in your daily routine.

৪৩

Our humanity leads us to spirituality, and spirituality deepens our humanity.

৪৩

Humanity is a beacon of kindness. The more humility you show outwardly, the greater joy you experience within.

৪৩

God's amazing grace flows effortlessly upon the pure gold of humility.

৪৩

I find peace focusing on the dark glow of the golden flame, where I see God's creation shining apart from the man-made world.

೫೦೧೩

I choose not to concern myself with the world's demands; I follow the voice of my heart.

೫೦೧೩

We are all shaped by our social surroundings, encountering different people in various ways and stages of life. Some are admired for their noble qualities and pleasant demeanour. Stay attentive as a listener, keeping your eyes and ears open to embrace their inspiring new ideas.

೫೦೧೩

No one's life is perfect, but we can fill our life with moments that make it feel perfect.

೫೦೧೩

Live life on your own terms, not according to others' expectations.

೫೦೧೩

Don't let your life be stuck in the past. Move forward and allow yourself to make each new day better than the last.

೫೦೧೩

Keep walking, because if you stop, your medicines will start walking with you.

છ

In life, there are three things you can never get back: words once spoken, moments once missed, and time once passed. A brilliant teacher is like hidden gold in a mine, uncovering possibilities beyond boundaries and leaving an impact that lasts forever.

છ

A teacher's role is to help students learn, but being a student goes beyond instruction. A student becomes their own best teacher by choosing the right path.

છ

Home is our first school, where we learn life's lessons and prepare for the tests of the outside world.

છ

Knowledge is readily available at the library, and gaining more of it has the power to transform your life forever.

છ

Align your knowledge with God, and it will yield the greatest rewards; peace and joy within.

છ

Integrity is not a gift but an achievement earned through hard work. It rests on a foundation of strong moral values, reflecting a person's wisdom and understanding.

౸౹

Fill your heart with uplifting emotions and the joy of simplicity as part of your daily life.

౸౹

By building on positive thoughts, you create your own little kingdom, where you govern with power and authority.

౸౹

Be as beloved as the sky, in love with the Sun and Moon, spreading light, harmony, and fostering healthy relationships to brighten the darkness, teaching strength and unity.

౸౹

Perform a kind act for someone, and you will also experience a deep sense of joy within.

౸౹

A mind centered and focused, like a supercomputer, is one of the most powerful forces in the universe.

౸౹

To earn more, you must first learn more.

ॐ

It's not education itself that's essential, but the knowledge it
imparts.

ॐ

Life is shaped by our emotions and knowledge. We make it
either bitter or better. In my view, life is always better when
we understand the bittersweet truths it holds.

ॐ

Curiosity is the most powerful source behind all inventions.

ॐ

Every struggle of today will shape you into a stronger
person tomorrow.

ॐ

Life isn't about going one way or another; it's about
working toward your goals, day by day.

ॐ

Patiently moving forward with quiet dedication is a
beautiful expression of emotion.

ॐ

Focus on changing yourself rather than trying to change others.

ॐ

Success lies in overcoming all obstacles.

ॐ

Persistent effort is the key to progress, and progress accelerates with time. Trust your life's journey, be patient, make healthy choices, and embrace your authentic self.

ॐ

Encouraging words are like oxygen for the human spirit, propelling people toward growth and success.

ॐ

Words carry great power. Choose them wisely to uplift and encourage others, rather than to bring them down.

ॐ

O God, inspire me today to speak kind, gentle words with respect, for tomorrow I may have to answer for them.

ॐ

Channel your mind into creative pursuits. Learn to play an instrument with dedication, and make music a larger part of your life, it's a purposeful way to train and discipline your mind.

ഇരു

Reading and writing are divine tools for enhancing focus, nourishing the body, and revitalizing the mind. Through this practice, I feel refreshed throughout the day, while learning new things. I cherish this sacred source as a beacon to illuminate my thoughts.

ഇരു

You must show your wisdom by applying the lessons you've gained from life experience.

ഇരു

The will of God is so kind, for He stands at our door as the Great Giver, continuously offering with open hands, sharing all that He has with everyone. Let us sing praises and give thanks for His everlasting love.

ഇരു

You don't need to rely solely on your own efforts for support or advancement. Don't be afraid—trust in God, for He is already working in your life with His blessings. Remember

this: when God opens doors for you, no force, whether
earthly or not, can stop your success.

ॐ

Rely on no one but God, for He is within you.

ॐ

The body is made up of five elements, a reflection of spirit
in action. It moves in harmony, dancing to the melodies of
both joy and sorrow.

ॐ

The unbreakable connection between body, mind, and
spirit shows that a positive mind, a pure heart, and a clear
conscience are essential for a healthy and prosperous life.

ॐ

Avoid becoming overly attached to anything, as attachment
is the source of all sufferings.

ॐ

The soul requires no teaching, only enlightenment.

ॐ

Turn off the light. Step into the darkness and illuminate the world with the lights of your being.

ॐ

Purify your heart and mind, and let your senses resonate in harmony with God as you play the instrument of life.

ॐ

As you sing of God's glory, say, 'Not my will, but Yours, O God,' and so it shall be.

ॐ

Align your knowledge with God, and it will yield the greatest return, inner peace and joy.

ॐ

Being in tune with God brings an overwhelming sense of inner peace. It is a reliable treasure chest of endless joy that guides us and blesses us continually.

ॐ

"Om" represents the divine essence of life, the sound that reverberates through the universe.

ॐ

Though the world is filled with chaos and contradictions,
divine harmony exists within it. I fill my mind with
the music of aspirations and play songs of faith on my
instrument, striving to live in harmony with the divine.

ॐ

Singing is a great exercise that boosts oxygen levels and
improves breathing. It helps relax the lungs, heart, and
body, while allowing rhythmic energy to flow naturally.

ॐ

I enjoy harmonizing with the infinite serenity of nature's
sounds, like enchanting music through which God speaks to
us in our own language, reminding us to stop seeking beauty
outside ourselves.

ॐ

I have a deep love for classical music and enjoy singing with
freedom.

ॐ

Being in harmony with God is so reliable that you can
place your entire life in His hands. God knows what is best
for us and provides at the right time. With God, all things
are possible. When our mind is aligned with Him, we will
always stay in sync with the melody of life.

ॐ

The best part about being a DJ is bringing happiness to people. There's nothing quite like watching people dance to different tunes, their rhythmic movements in harmony with the music, unleashing their full potential.

₧₧

The outer world is crafted by God, and when we freely express our imagination, we realize that love is life's greatest refreshment, creating a balanced harmony that makes the whole world sing.

₧₧

Life is a beautiful canvas on which we paint the shades of our soul with deliberate strokes, forming a glowing image that stands as tangible proof of beauty within a single frame.

₧₧

Every artist's goal is to capture the motions of their imaginative mind and engage in a philosophical dance of ideas through creative hands. The finest art, viewed through disciplined eyes, reflects an inner perspective on life. The artist preserves this vision so that, even centuries later, when others gaze upon it, the work still shines and continues to inspire minds.

₧₧

Whether I find myself in deep thought, love, or joy, I feel fortunate to be able to express my emotions through poetry.

ಸಂ

When my mind aligns with my thoughts, my heart believes, and my inner voice whispers, "Ah!" leading my soul to a state of heavenly fulfillment.

ಸಂ

I prefer to enjoy the moment so fully that no time is left for anything else.

ಸಂ

I often put my inner feelings into writing, and it's truly a source of inspiration for me. While I may seem extroverted by nature, I'm an introvert at heart. I cherish spending time with myself, as it nurtures my creativity. I find happiness in simply being with me.

ಸಂ

A heart filled with peace and joy, a stable mind, and a soul full of love creates a whole being of light. Spiritual growth brings ever-renewing joy.

ಸಂ

Happiness is a state of mind and emotion, marked by a
deep sense of inner joy and contentment.

ഇറ

Cultivate a heart full of blossoms and become the ruler of
your own inner kingdom.

ഇറ

My soul is already a garden of blooming flowers—why look
for happiness anywhere else?

ഇറ

I'm captivated by the beauty of flowers, which fill my heart
with joy and expand my mind as they bloom. Their silent
message to me is clear, sing a quiet song of love.

ഇറ

Blooming flowers perform a rhythmic dance, like Romeo
and Juliet, releasing the fragrant essence of joy, love, and
peace. This radiant beauty completes my wholeness and
rejuvenates my spirit.

ഇറ

The dancing flowers are so enthralling that everyone stays
awake, enchanted by their silent love songs.

ഇറ

Cultivate a garden of awakening blooms in your heart,
nourishing it with love, humility, patience, and persistence.
One day, you will witness the long-awaited blessings of
these flowers blooming within your mortal grace.

৪৩

A bird sings instinctively, and as I listen closely to its
melodic, rhythmic notes, a natural symphony blossoms
within my consciousness.

৪৩

The bird of life soars through time, carried by the wind,
never pausing, always moving forward until the breath
ceases and the wings fall still. In the end, the bird of life
departs from the body's cage.

৪৩

Once life has departed, the body is left behind, unnoticed,
as all desire to lay it to rest in the earth.

৪৩

Each moment flies by, like a feather on the broad wings of
time, so don't let yourself fall behind.

৪৩

The incredible flight of birds teaches me to be like them—master the art of soaring, maintain perfect balance, and spread the wings of my free will. Embrace life with effort and joy, sing in harmony with the sunlight, and fly with the universe, loving the sky and embracing the freedom of an airborne existence.

৪৩

We will all face death someday, but no one can predict the time, date, month, or year. It could come at any moment, at any age, when we least expect it. We must accept it as part of life's eternal cycle.

৪৩

In a single moment, death erases the very essence of life's presence, reminding us of the fragility and impermanence of existence. It urges us to cherish each moment, live with purpose, and leave a lasting impact, for our time is finite and unpredictable.

৪৩

Death can't be delayed or avoided by saying it's in the distant future; in many ways, we experience small deaths repeatedly. It's better to release the things that cause sadness and focus on living fully and dreaming boldly. Remember, we only get one life.

৪৩

Since the day I was born, death has been approaching me. I ask it, "Hello there, when will you come for me?" Death replies, "I'm in no rush. Live a joyful and peaceful life, so I can bring you a peaceful and joyful death."

෫ඏ

I will leave this Earth with joy, carrying a sense of fulfillment and peace, hoping never to return again. In that departure, I seek liberation from the burdens of this world, trusting that the journey ahead holds new beginnings, free from the cycles of past experiences. My legacy will remain, but my soul will move forward, embracing the unknown with a heart full of gratitude.

෫ඏ

Self-realization changes us, shedding our old, desire-driven selves and dressing us in a new identity, cleansed by the purifying light of invaluable knowledge.

෫ඏ

In life, we encounter many people, some are lovable, dignified, reliable, and kind, while others are deceitful, unreasonable, and quick to hurt. You can rise above such negativity by maintaining politeness.

෫ඏ

Many people criticize the world, hoping to change it, but they rarely consider changing themselves. Through love

and understanding, working together, they can transform
their environment—and maybe even the world. Changing
yourself is the first step to change the world.

৪০০৪

The universe is abundant with remarkable individuals,
though not everyone shines immediately. Some take time to
grow into their full potential, but in time, everyone will find
their light and rise to it.

৪০০৪

In moments of mental calm, I discover the truth: "If I
have peace within, the entire universe is peaceful. If I find
happiness in each moment, the universe becomes a source of
joy. If I love myself, others will love me too."

৪০০৪

Our greatest flaw as humans is that we only half-listen to
what is said, understand even less, and yet we act as though
we know it all.

৪০০৪

The more you learn, the more you enrich your own
understanding. The more you teach, the deeper your
learning becomes, enhancing both your knowledge and your
ability to grow.

৪০০৪

Learn to carry yourself with honour, as every truly decent human being should.

૭૦૦૨

Choose friends not based on their appearance, but for their empathy and understanding.

૭૦૦૨

Don't follow the crowd, be the one they follow.

૭૦૦૨

Don't let the world change you, transform yourself from within.

૭૦૦૨

Lead a simple and balanced life, for the laws of the universe are simple.

૭૦૦૨

Be a beacon of light, offering hope and life to someone in their darkest times.

૭૦૦૨

It is our moral responsibility to prioritize God in our lives, with everything else coming after.

૭૦૦૨

Through meditation and stillness before God, you can
clarify your perception of reality. God is our only refuge,
and His presence constantly brings a joyful flow to our lives.

ഇ൯ഝ

Build a vision for your life driven by passion, not status, and
watch how clarity unfolds moment by moment. It's simpler
than it seems.

ഇ൯ഝ

Keep your mind open, for it sees with countless eyes. If you
close it, nothing will be possible for you to envision.

ഇ൯ഝ

My vision enables me to see the world's potential and turn
my dreams into reality.

ഇ൯ഝ

I always focus on the positive side of things and help them
flourish.

ഇ൯ഝ

Break free from your limited mindset. Step forward, move
on. Every step you take brings you closer to something
greater than where you are now.

ഇ൯ഝ

 INWARD REFLECTIONS

Don't rely on others to navigate life. Stand tall! Learn to take steps on your own. Only you can transform your life through your excitement and experiences.

ഇരുമ

Commit to self-education and focus on continuous self-discovery and improvement.

ഇരുമ

Simply being alive isn't enough. What matters is how deeply you connect with the wonders of life.

ഇരുമ

Stay so engaged that you have no time to judge or criticize others.

ഇരുമ

The flaws you see in others often reflect your own.

ഇരുമ

When others criticize my lifestyle and personal philosophy, I don't let it affect me, it actually fuels my constructive energy.

ഇരുമ

Present yourself with confidence to showcase your charismatic style and leave a lasting first impression.

ಬಂಧ

My future starts with the break of dawn. Each day, I decide to engage in creative pursuits.

ಬಂಧ

I look in the mirror and say, "Mirror, you are perfect in your own way, always reflecting honesty without needing words."

ಬಂಧ

Swap your old lifestyle for a new one. Take a chance, try something different, and shift your consciousness where it's needed most.

ಬಂಧ

Namaste acknowledges the infinite within me, honouring the infinite within you. I bow to that divinity.

ಬಂಧ

Nature is God's ever-flowing gift. I love to walk in the beauty of this divine creation.

ಬಂಧ

Be the master of yourself, directing your actions as needed, while letting go of unproductive thoughts and habits.

ಜಲ

Time spent in the uplifting presence of God will infuse you with harmony and inspire noble thoughts within.

ಜಲ

Every moment is a good one if you know how to make the most of it, in the right place and time.

ಜಲ

The rhythm of harmony always walks with me, enhancing my wholeness and refreshing my spirit. That makes me Sing.

ಜಲ

The struggles of your past shape the future you build.

ಜಲ

Let the past stay where it belongs, and it will release you into the present.

ಜಲ

We only live once. Make the most of every moment by doing good, and in doing so, your name will be remembered for eternity.

෨෬

In today's world, where disappointment and insecurity weigh heavily on people, many walk with uncertainty in their steps, smiles, and minds. At this point, turning to God and practicing meditation is the path to purifying the mind.

෨෬

Greatness comes from one's intense passion, not just from effort.

෨෬

True success is born from deep, reflective thinking.

෨෬

No matter how successful people become, they gain power and respect through humility. They see their greatness modestly.

෨෬

I deeply admire great intellectuals who are gifted with insight, and with heartfelt honesty, choose to shine after enduring life's storms, darkness, and complexity.

෨෬

Walking alongside a leader helps develop leadership within you.

ॐ

Time spent with great individuals instils confidence and inspires you to become a person of action. In contrast, small-minded people slow down your ambitions, so keep your distance from them.

ॐ

Surround yourself with people who possess strong minds and a positive outlook. This will greatly improve your life.

ॐ

Knowledge and wisdom gained through personal experience and observation are far more valuable than knowledge from books.

ॐ

Knowledge is useless unless it is put into practice.

ॐ

I view the world with the understanding that everyone is on a journey of discovery through their experiences.

ॐ

Behind one small candle lies a powerful force capable of lighting thousands more. Similarly, our minds can ignite the light in others through the inspiration of our thoughts, words, and actions.

℘℮

Just as one candle lights thousands, a single flash of wisdom can enlighten countless minds.

℘℮

Don't care what people say about you. Just follow your heart and spread good vibes wherever you go.

℘℮

Good people are driven by the ambition to serve others cheerfully, becoming a "Torch of Truth" that brightens even the darkest places.

℘℮

Present yourself by offering a helping hand to those in need, with sincerity and humility. This is one of the most profound forms of worship and a lifestyle rooted in love and healing.

℘℮

Worship is meaningless if your neighbour is hungry.

℘℮

 INWARD REFLECTIONS

Be kind to everyone, even if someone has betrayed your love and trust. Don't worry, stay true to yourself, as that is the most genuine way to live wisely.

ॐ

Let us become a valley of smiles, flourishing with happiness and harmony.

ॐ

Cheerfulness is a mindset, a spiritual aspiration that brings an indescribable joy to life.

ॐ

A cheerful mind is like a garden of blooming flowers, spreading sweet fragrance and joy to everyone within its reach.

ॐ

The sweet magic of a cheerful presence brightens the hearts of the neglected and frustrated, scattering joyful rays from within.

ॐ

Spread happiness wherever you go. Smile, it costs nothing but gives so much.

ॐ

Keep the control of your happiness in your own hands, not in someone else's.

ॐ

Laughter is a healthy, welcoming emotional expression that transcends caste and religion. It is the universal language of the world.

ॐ

Cheerfulness is the best remedy for health, especially when combined with right thinking and right living.

ॐ

A genuine smile can bring about positive changes in life's well-being.

ॐ

Understanding creates harmony and balance in everyone's attitude.

ॐ

In my search for myself, I discovered the path of truth. That led me to love, and in love, I found everlasting joy and peace.

ॐ

 INWARD REFLECTIONS

Envision possibilities beyond the limits.

৪৩

A problem only becomes one because of our attitude toward
it.

৪৩

Free your mind from the dust of ego, dear friend. Clear
away ego's grip, and everything will become clearer.

৪৩

Put your ego aside and cultivate the valuable skill of
politeness.

৪৩

Don't let your ego get too close, or it will undermine your
abilities and bring you down.

৪৩

The core of ego is the "I," focused only on itself. But if ego
takes a moment to look around, it will see that the universe
is an extension of God's love, flowing freely. When ego
realizes this, it will dissolve into love and cease to exist.

৪৩

Strive to turn the impossible into reality.

৹৻৻

If you believe in tension, it will strike back. If you don't,
you'll conquer it.

৹৻৻

Perceptions vary, what seems positive to some may seem
negative to others.

৹৻৻

It's not the muscles that burn; it's the inner drive that fuels
the fire.

৹৻৻

Don't cut down trees; they provide shelter for birds under
their shade.

৹৻৻

Don't waste your precious time in thinking about those
things you have missed in your life. Focus on what you have.

৹৻৻

I don't need much; I just want to live a happy, stress-free life.

৹৻৻

Worry doesn't prevent bad things; it only stops you from
enjoying the good.

ॐ

In tough times, don't lose hope. Pray to God, you never
know when His blessings will flow into your life.

ॐ

When life pulls you down, God's grace lifts you up. Trust
Him completely, for His protection is always present.

ॐ

Trust in your ability to handle the stress that life brings.

ॐ

Crying is better than anger, which can wound others. Tears
silently cleanse the heart, while anger causes harm.

ॐ

We should envy no one. Let others envy the unique abilities
and lifestyle that we possess.

ॐ

Life is a canvas on which we carefully paint the shades
of our soul, creating a glowing masterpiece that captures
beauty in a single frame.

ॐ

Amid the noise of life, I hear many sounds, but I choose
to hold onto the melodious ones and forget the bitterness. I
embrace the beauty of the natural world—stars, the sun, the
moon, and planets capture my attention, and their beauty
stays with me. It's only through practical experience that I
learn new techniques.

ॐ

Solitude refreshes my soul. I cherish my peaceful loneliness
and find supreme bliss within.

ॐ

Life is as sweet as we allow it to be.

ॐ

Live each day as if it's your last. Take time to enjoy life and
relish the sweet fragrance of flowers.

ॐ

Life is happening now. Now is the time, the hour, the day.
There is no later, there is only the present.

ॐ

Our time on earth is limited. Don't waste it worrying about others' opinions that disrupt your inner peace. Let go of the things that don't matter.

৪৩

Focus on positive thoughts and solutions. Uplift your soul, this is what truly matters in life.

৪৩

What we hold in our minds will eventually manifest in reality.

৪৩

It's not just about doing your work; it's about how well you do it that truly matters.

৪৩

Everyone cherishes the canopy of an umbrella in both sunshine and rain, as it feels like a divine blessing in moments of need.

৪৩

Play your part on the stage of time, enjoying all the resources available to you. Leave your legacy through your words and virtuous deeds.

৪৩

Our destiny is crafted by the choices we make in our work
and the emotional decisions we take.

৪৩

Don't tell your problem to anyone as people pretend to not
have ears.

৪৩

Create a garden of happiness and noble thoughts in
your life. Fill it with the fragrance of love and beautiful
experiences, and enjoy everlasting peace and harmony
inside and out.

৪৩

When we achieve fulfillment within, the external world
transforms, bringing greater joy and lasting peace.

৪৩

You can't please everyone all the time, so make it your goal
to please God and find contentment within yourself.

৪৩

No life is perfect, but we can fill it with moments that make
it feel perfect.

৪৩

We live in a world of illusions, where everything seems so captivating that we mistake it for reality. But what we see is merely an illusion. The true reality lies in finding joy within ourselves.

ೀ

Illusions are a powerful magnet that draw us to everything around us.

ೀ

Life isn't meant to follow a set path; instead, you must work toward your goals day by day.

ೀ

It's not about how many times we fall, but how many times we rise again. That's the essence of life—the drama of ups and downs.

ೀ

Every struggle of today will shape you into a stronger person of tomorrow.

ೀ

A person who finds contentment in poverty is happier than one with wealth but no joy.

ೀ

A person who holds inner contentment is connected to their
own inner heaven.

හ)ශ

We are all reflections of God, who loves us equally. Follow
God and live with a free spirit, embracing all without
discrimination, that's what makes us truly human.

හ)ශ

Every human has incredible abilities within, let yours shine.

හ)ශ

Don't wait for things to happen. Make them happen with
bold, graceful actions. Tap into your inner intelligence and try
something new, you can create change right here and now.

හ)ශ

Living in the present moment is the true art of life. Focus
your mind on this moment with wisdom and sincerity, it
holds the key to all others.

හ)ශ

Make your world sparkle like a diamond. Shine as brightly
as gold, fill your heart with grace like an emerald, and keep
your soul pure like a pearl. Live and love with brilliance, no
matter your age.

හ)ශ

Live by these four principles: Love, Serve, Courage, and
Faith. Reflect deeply on them to bring positive results.

☙❧

Who you are inside will eventually be reflected on the
outside.

☙❧

A gentle reminder to myself: breathe deeply and relax.
Everything around me, whether good or bad, is temporary.
To live joyfully, I embrace moments of dance, music,
creativity, healthy eating, and wearing nice clothes. I make
the most of what matters to me and say, "Thank God
for everything." I let go of what doesn't matter and find
satisfaction in what I have.

☙❧

I spend a lot of time searching for myself through reading
and writing. When I write, I lose myself in words, and
unspoken thoughts take literary form in my mind. I express
my journey with gentle language, organize my thoughts, and
leave the rest to God.

☙❧

Whatever experiences come our way, it's our understanding
or misunderstanding that turns a moment into heaven or hell.

☙❧

I've faced difficult times in life, feeling alone in my darkest moments. But I kept life interesting with a positive outlook, sparkling eyes, and a radiant smile that got me through and made me feel special.

❧☙

A long trip to the mall is my go-to energy booster. In search of joy, I love spending money on fabulous, stylish clothes for my closet. My elegant, sophisticated style keeps me both physically and mentally fit.

❧☙

I cherish long, loving relationships where I can spend more and more time. Letting go of grudges and bitterness makes room for joy and connection, giving me a sense of purpose in life.

❧☙

When I pause to connect with my breath, I remind myself, "Yes, I'm alive." And with that, I know everything is fine.

❧☙

Sometimes I wonder, "What is life? Where do we come from? Why are we here? Why do we endure such pain?" No one knows the answers. Then I remind myself, "Life isn't here to be questioned; it's here to be lived."

❧☙

 INWARD REFLECTIONS

Life is a gift, and my purpose is to be authentically myself.

૪૦૦૨

My life feels like a beautiful movie. I play the lead role and experience reality, with God as the director. I love my role as the hero, striving to perform it well through good karma and effort. I may not always succeed, but I win the award of peace, contentment, and harmony. I don't become the role, I immerse myself in it.

૪૦૦૨

What we do in our private world is what we call life.

૪૦૦૨

I'm the curator of my own life, balancing my plans in the palm of my hand.

૪૦૦૨

Celebrate your life by creating your own magic. Let your inner self inspire and encourage you.

૪૦૦૨

My joyful lifestyle and sense of style keep me in tune with others. It's clear my friends enjoy my company and I trust their judgment.

૪૦૦૨

God is the creator of all things, and we are just part of His creation. We have no right to harm anything that we did not create.

৪৩

God made this earth for us to live, love, and find joy and faith, not for worry and fear. So, breathe freely and let go of fear.

৪৩

It's not about how often we fall, but how many times we rise again. That's the essence of life's drama, ups and downs.

৪৩

A sincere smile can make everything seem brighter.

৪৩

True success is born from deep, thoughtful reflection.

৪৩

Cultivate a garden of happiness and noble thoughts. Fill it with love and beautiful experiences, and bask in the everlasting peace and harmony both inside and out.

৪৩

Our moral responsibility is to prioritize God in our lives,
leaving everything else to follow.

80C8

With every step, we learn something new. Learning is a
continuous journey.

80C8

Banish negativity by shining the light of positive thinking.

80C8

Peace and love are deeply felt in both the heart and mind.

80C8

True love awakens joy, moving the soul to dance not just
with the hands, but with the heart.

80C8

My agile mindset is built on simple principles and
philosophy, keeping me energized with self-discipline.

80C8

Faith in God brings forth light, and that light is His
presence.

80C8

Stay grounded, for one day all lives must ascend.

೮೦೦೪

The human body is a melodic instrument. Our goal is to stay in tune with God's frequency and enjoy the sweet music of His presence, both inside and out.

೮೦೦೪

Humility is the highest virtue of love. It creates a powerful, transformative way of life that can heal the world holistically.

೮೦೦೪

Trust is essential, and loyalty is like royalty. To me both are commendable qualities.

೮೦೦೪

Loyalty builds trust. Trust brings stability. Stability fosters love, and love gives birth to hope. Hope is the voice of inspiration. You can hear its whispers if you believe.

೮೦೦೪

Why don't we live in peace? If we all strive for peace, we can turn our families into blooming flowers, our societies, cities, and eventually our nation will flourish in peace.

೮೦೦೪

Free your mind from frustration, stress, anger, tension, and ego. Create space for positive experiences and, in doing so, win the jackpot of spontaneous peace, beauty, happiness, and love.

ॐ

Enjoying my own company is part of who I am. My cheerful nature is grounded in reality.

ॐ

Don't carry the burden of expectations, they often lead to disappointment and grief.

ॐ

Life is short, so let joy flow freely. It's the best energy boost.

ॐ

Today will pass, tomorrow will fade, but each day brings its own gentle sense of life.

ॐ

Break free from your confined mindset. Take steps forward, each one brings you closer to something greater than where you are now.

ॐ

Women don't need special treatment to reach great heights, they need equality. And if they aren't given it, they'll still succeed without any help. But trust me, they will succeed.

లు౭

I don't enjoy unnecessary drama wasting my time, but during tough times, my true friends bring light-hearted humour that makes me laugh. In those moments, the trivial drama fills me with joy and peace.

లు౭

I live well through my actions; I'm doing just fine. My real performance makes people wonder, how I keep smiling even when there are tears in my eyes.

లు౭

Solitude is where I find the strength to continue with life. I love the sensitive person within me, and it's important that I nurture my inner vitality and love through meditation.

లు౭

To align my thoughts with God, I make Him part of every moment. I never feel lonely because God is always with me, providing all that I need.

లు౭

 INWARD REFLECTIONS

God's Word is always active in this world. Take a moment
to listen.

ೲ

Achievements reflect the great desire, devotion, and
dedication of the achiever.

ೲ

Walk your path like a train, straightforward, without turning
or stopping until you reach your destination.